Blood ...

Life in paradise can drive you buggy! Your body is just another link in the mosquito's food chain. You've got to share your home with relentless roaches, your yard with ferocious fire ants, and your car with lascivious love bugs.

Sweat ...

Man may have discovered Florida, but God made the air conditioner! Sure it adds a few hundred dollars to your monthly electric bill, but without it you would look like a sweaty Redi-Killowatt.

Tears ...

Debby Wood's rollicking tales of life in Florida are sure to bring tears of laughter. With her irreverent humor and delightful style, she takes a real slice at paradise.

Also by Debby Wood:

"Oh, God not another beautiful day!"
Middle age & other spreads

Debby Wood's

Florida

A Slice of
Paradise

1
Florida: a state for all seasons

A lot of visitors from the north think that Florida has no seasons. Ha! What do they know?

True, the leaves on the coconut palms don't turn bright red on October 1 and drop to the ground in November. And tulips don't push up through the sand in April to announce the arrival of Spring. But that doesn't mean Florida lacks seasons.

The way I see it, there are four distinct seasons in the sunshine state. We have the wet season, the dry season, the tourist season and the air-conditioning season. If that's not enough, we have several mini-seasons, like the love bug season and the mosquito season. And sometimes we have the red tide season.

The wet season is easy to identify. When you look out your window one afternoon in June and notice the sky turning the color of India ink, you know that the wet season is about to begin.

In case you don't recognize the wet season by the five or six inches of rain that fall nearly every day, there are other clues. You know it's the wet season when you have to cut your grass every third day and when the swimming pool is continuously at the flood level stage.

You can expect to find mildew under your pillow when you wake up in the morning, and you can hear the rust eating away at your car when you stop at a red light. The shower curtain never completely dries out, even when you go away for a week's vacation.

During this time of year, lightning invariably causes a power outage just about the time you are ready to fix dinner, forcing you to do a lot of barbecuing and eating by candlelight.

If you notice a lot of people carrying umbrellas on an otherwise sunny afternoon, you can bet it's the wet season. Another clue: If there is a parade of boats racing up the river from the Gulf between noon and 3 p.m., you can probably assume they are heading for dry dock.

The wet season brings out the things that go OOZE in the night, like snails, and slugs, and those really disgusting little frogs that stare at you through the window in the evening and sometimes end up dead in the bottom of the pool (where they belong). And mosquitoes reproduce like crazy, realizing that the wet season is their one and only opportunity to take over the world.

Sometime between Halloween and Christmas, the dry season gets underway. If it hasn't rained for more than seven days in succession, you can presume that the dry season has begun.

During the first two months of the dry season, people are always in a good mood, talking about how nice it is not to have to worry about those terrible rain storms anymore. During the last two months of the dry season, people are always near hysteria, talking about how Florida is going to dry up and become another Sahara Desert. They even contemplate sacrifices, like giving up clean cars or flushing every other time.

It's easy to recognize the dry season. Front yards turn the color of shoe leather, and about the same texture. Flowers and shrubbery tend to droop, and people water their lawns after dark so nobody will know.

If you live on a canal, you'll notice that your property seems a lot higher during the dry season. And boats have a tendency to run aground a lot more during this time of year.

For some strange reason, the tourist season generally coincides with the worst part of the dry season. The tourist season starts when the temperature in Ohio reaches the freezing mark. It builds slowly, but in February and March, Florida's two coldest months, millions of tourists flock to the beaches while the residents huddle under blankets at home.

I'll never understand why tourists pick the worst time of year to visit our state. Maybe that's the only time they can find room on the beaches.

Every once in a while we may experience a "freeze" during the tourist season. While a freeze is bad for the farmers, it's good for the store owners because most tourists decide to spend their time shopping instead of swimming in 60 degree water.

During a freeze, only tourists from Manitoba swim in the Gulf. And that's when local newspaper photographers dressed in fur-lined parkas and mittens drive out to the beach to take pictures of those crazy tourists who don't know they're supposed to be huddled up under blankets back in the motel.

Aside from the weather, there are other indications of the tourist season. You can't get a reservation in a restaurant. The highways are so crowded that it takes twice as long to get anywhere. And if you stop at the post office to buy a stamp, they may have raised the postage rate by the time you get to the front of the line.

The tourist season ends abruptly right after Easter, just when the weather in Florida gets really nice. If the tourists ever knew what they were missing, they might extend the season. But that would destroy the balance of nature.

The longest (and newest) season in Florida is the air-conditioning season. It was created by the electric company in the 1950s to boost sagging profits, and since its inception it has been quite successful.

3

The air-conditioning season starts in June, just about the time the wet season makes the humidity unbearable. But it is interesting to note that as the price of electricity goes up each year, the season starts later and later.

During this season most people stay inside, just as they do during the winter up north. Neighbors lose track of one another and children never play in the street. Suntans fade. The only people with any coloring are the occasional tourists.

How can you tell if it's air-conditioning season? Your hair frizzes in the time it takes you to get from your front door to your air-conditioned car. The porch furniture is covered with more mildew than the shower curtain.

A parked car turns into an oven. Open the door after a little shopping trip and the blast of hot air will knock you over. The steering wheel feels like it just came out of the furnace at U.S. Steel.

Silk flower arrangements come to life—with mold. The candles on the patio take on exotic new shapes and colors. The air conditioner in your car breaks every few weeks from overuse. Freon becomes the most valuable product in Florida.

If it takes you an extra 20 minutes to get dried off after your morning shower, chances are pretty good that air-conditioning season is at hand. It's the time of year when you switch to extra-strength deodorant.

Some people in Florida don't observe air-conditioning season. More power to them (and us). But to me, that's like hiking in the Everglades without a can of mosquito repellant. I'd rather die!

Who says Florida doesn't have seasons? It's a state for all seasons.

About the only season we don't have in Florida is the Christmas season, unless, of course, you can get into the holiday spirit by hanging twinkle lights on a cactus plant and pretending the white sand is really snow. Personally, I haven't been here long enough to get to that point!

2

If the shoe fits, you haven't been in Florida long enough!

I came to Florida wearing a pair of 7-narrow shoes. Today I can barely fit my foot into a 9-extra-wide moccasin.

It's been a gradual process, but over the past few years my feet have spread out in every direction, sort of like Heinz ketchup flowing out of the bottle . . . slowly, but surely.

There's only one thing to blame—the barefoot lifestyle of Florida.

For the first 32 years of my life my feet were stuffed into booties, high-tops, Oxfords, saddle shoes, sneakers, riding boots, loafers, Capezios, pumps and designer boots. And when they weren't in some sort of shoe, my feet were snuggly nestled inside some sort of slipper.

All that changed when I hit Florida. After all, the sunshine state is *made* for bare feet, isn't it? And if you can't go barefoot, flip-flops or sandals are suitable for nearly every occasion.

While my shoes have gathered dust in the far corner of the closet, I have gone through several pair of sandals each year. But without the walls of those shoes holding my feet firmly in shape, they have slowly collapsed like a bowl of warm Jello.

I've known what was happening all along, but I wasn't

aware how bad things had become until I went shopping for a pair of dressy shoes.

"I'd like to see these in a 7-narrow," I told the saleswoman, pointing to a pair of blue heels.

She looked at me, her eyebrow raised suspiciously, and said, "Maybe we better measure your foot. It looks a little large for a 7-narrow."

How rude! Why don't they teach these people some tact?

"Just as I thought," she said. "We better try an 8-medium." And she scurried into the far reaches of the shoe storage area before I could protest.

The shoe she came back with must have been mislabeled. Either that or there was a wad of tissue paper jammed into the toe. To say that it was uncomfortable is a gross understatement.

"Let me get a larger size," she said.

"Hold it, honey," I said, grabbing her by the arm. "Maybe this shoe isn't the right style for me."

"But this is the latest design. Everyone is wearing them."

"Don't you have anything with a lower heel and a wider toe? Maybe the sides could be a little stretchy? And a little more padding on the bottom?"

"How about this?" she said, holding up a shoe that must have been designed for Twiggy before she put on all that weight.

"I couldn't squeeze half my piggies into that shoe! Just where do you think I'm going to put my big toe?"

"Well, here's something with an open toe," she said.

"Yes, but look at that heel. It's so high I'd get a nosebleed. And so thin at the bottom I'd tip over."

"Well . . ." she said, looking around the store.

"How about these," I said, pointing to a pair of low-heeled shoes in the corner.

"I'm sorry, but they don't come in a size wide enough for your foot." She was cruel, there's no doubt about it!

I finally settled on some shoes that looked like sandals with slightly high heels.

"That'll be $89.95 plus tax," she said.

"WHAT! HOW MUCH?"

Everybody in the store was suddenly looking at me.

"$89.95," she said quietly.

"For a few strips of leather and a little heel?" I said in a voice loud enough for everyone in the store to hear.

I handed the shoe box back to her and walked out of the store, thinking how lucky I was that I didn't have to buy a lot of shoes every year.

Besides, no one will notice that I'm wearing my flip-flops at a formal dance. I'll just glue some sequins on the thongs and paint my toenails. And if anyone complains, I can always go barefoot.

3
The bug stops here

My lawn will never be listed in *"Famous Lawns of America."* Unless, of course, they have a chapter on disasters to avoid.

Five years ago the lawn was a luscious carpet of green grass . . . the talk of the neighborhood. Then came an invasion of mole crickets, and in no time the lawn-spraying companies were making pests out of themselves trying to save my lawn.

They failed.

Those little mole crickets were just too smart. When they caught a glimpse of the pest control people, they would scamper across the street and hang out in the vacant lot until it was safe to return home.

Within a few months we were on a first-name basis with the mole crickets. I tried to negotiate with them to save the lawn, but one of them told me they didn't believe in collective bargaining.

Finally I resorted to armed warfare. Do you realize how silly a grown woman looks crawling on her hands and knees, pounding the ground with a hammer? Some of the neighbors still steer clear of me!

The hammer nailed a few mole crickets, but it was too late. By the time the fear of "the hatchet lady" spread in the mole cricket community, they had eaten out the roots of nearly the entire yard and were heading for another lawn.

9

Faced with the choice of living the rest of our lives in the middle of a giant sand trap or resodding the yard, my husband chose a cheaper route. He brought home a few pieces of Floratam sod, nestled them into the sand at strategic places, and said something like "Don't worry, we'll have a beautiful lawn by this time next year."

That was in 1979. Today those little pieces of sod have spread to at least three times their original size. In fact, in the back yard there's an area of grass that's big enough to set up a lawn chair, if you don't mind sticking your feet in the sand.

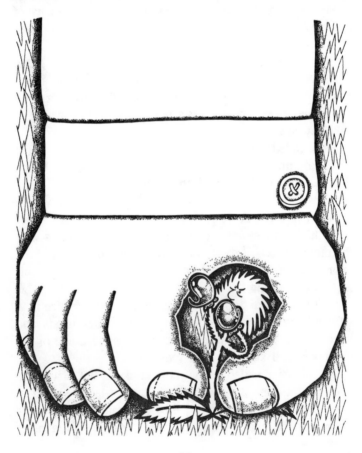

And while I haven't seen a mole cricket in at least three years, we now have a new enemy to battle—the fire ant.

Fire ants are nasty little creatures. Not only are they vicious, they're vindictive. Anyone who disturbs a colony of fire ants will live to regret it.

The tenacious red insects first invaded our front yard. My husband thought they were easy to control. Little did he know that the poison he spread on those little ant hills acted more like vitamins for the fire ants.

In no time at all we had mounds of fire ants popping up all over the yard. And when one colony of ants abandons a mound and goes looking for greener pastures, the old mound dries out and inevitably turns into something harder than concrete.

The ants are pests in another way. They bite!

One little fire ant can latch onto you with a set of teeth that rivals the shark in Jaws. And while the ant holds onto your leg, he stings you repeatedly. Talk about painful!

What's worse, you usually don't know you've been standing on a family of fire ants until a dozen are crawling up your thigh. Then one of them shouts "vengeance is mine," and they all start biting at the same time.

As I was buying our weekly supply of Mirex (the giant economy bag), I started telling the garden center man my tale of woe.

His advice: Learn to live with them.

Never!

I've ordered a South American anteater. If that doesn't keep the fire ants at bay, I'm going to wave the white flag, put a "for sale" sign up in the only green spot left in the front yard, and head north. Let them win the war by default.

4
The garden gets even

You can always tell which people are the new residents in Florida. They're the ones in the garden centers buying the bougainvillea plants.

Nobody who has ever tried to prune a bougainvillea bush would seriously consider buying another one. The thorns are about the size of hypodermic needles, and a lot more painful. And the branches grow faster than kudzu.

During our first month in Florida, my husband bought three bougainvillea plants in assorted colors. He's cursed the day ever since. Every few months he prunes the bushes to within an inch of their lives. They always bounce back, much to his dismay.

But for those new residents strolling through the garden center for the first time, the beautiful bougainvillea flowers are too tempting to pass up.

It's funny how people who move to Florida seem to spend the first few months buying plants and garden supplies. Even if the home they buy is beautifully land-scaped, they just can't resist buying a few more plants and trees. I guess after spending a lifetime in Ohio, it's hard to resist buying a gardenia plant or an orange tree.

But watch out. There's a law in Florida that requires all plants to grow to abnormal proportions as soon as they're taken out of their pots. Newcomers should be warned that a twig casually stuck in the ground can become a six-foot bush by the end of the summer, and a full-grown tree in another year.

So I'd like to go over a few of the plants you should definitely avoid when you're wandering down those long paths at the nursery.

Crown of thorns: These attractive plants look beautiful in a pot, but once they're in the ground, those prickly branches stretch out in your garden, and there's not much that won't get out of the way. In a matter of months baby bushes start sprouting up throughout your garden, and soon you have an entire bed of thorns. Pruning can be done only when wearing heavy asbestos gloves, lined with steel fingertips. You have to be a saint to put up with the crown of thorns.

Oleander: Beautiful clusters of colorful flower make this plant particularly desirable for your yard. But you should be aware that the plant is poisonous to everything but tiny furry caterpillars, which reproduce at an alarming rate. The caterpillars consume great quantities of oleander leaves, often leaving only the stems of the plant.

Cactus: Nobody in their right mind should ever consider planting one of those large cactus plants with the spikes on the end that look like ice picks. The plants are lethal! Anyone sadistic enough to want such a weapon should be required to register it with the police department. Once the cactus is established, it will be there for the rest of eternity. You can't get rid of it, no matter how many times you wound yourself while cutting grass. But you're in luck if a large stalk starts growing out of the center of the cactus. The stalk shoots toward the sky at a frightening speed and surely must have been the model for Jack and the Beanstalk. When it is 40 or 50 feet tall, strange looking flowers appear on top, and the rest of the cactus starts to turn brown. Then, and only then, can you cut it down and pull the cactus out by its roots, unless, of course, you like having a telephone pole with flowers on the top growing in your front yard. If you're stuck with the cactus, you can always cut out the bottom of an egg carton and stick the little foam flowers on the tips of the cactus. It's tacky, but it's safe.

Brazilian pepper: Plant one of these babies and you won't have to worry about cutting the grass, weeding the garden or pruning the shrubs. In no time at all you will have Brazilian pepper trees all over your property. They're kind of like rabbits—they reproduce and they grow big, fast. The birds love to eat the berries, get drunk, and then pretend they're B-52s, dive-bombing through your screen enclosure and then drowning in your pool.

Ferns: Lovely to look at, ferns can take over your garden before you know it. Their little runners can sneak under the sidewalk, through your patio screening, between your sliding glass windows, into your house and down into your garbage disposal. They don't know when to stop. By the way, potted ferns on your patio can make cleaning the pool a real challenge.

Tomatoes: Unless you want to grow a healthy crop of bugs in your garden, you can forget about growing tomatoes in Florida. By the time they're juicy and red, the bugs have eaten them from the inside out.

Seagrape trees: Although these trees have a lot going for them, there is one serious drawback. Every year the leaves fall off. And the leaves are so big that if you don't get out of the way, you're likely to get a concussion if one hits you. You can't rake seagrape leaves, you have to pick them up, one by one. About 20 leaves will fill up your garbage can.

Vines: Last but not least, vines can cover up all your other landscaping mistakes. One little leftover vine from a discarded dish garden can destroy your entire garden in just one wet summer. And once the vine takes root, there's no way to win the battle. You might as well just sell the house and move while you can still get out the front door!

5
Confessions of a semi-native

You know you've been in Florida too long when your daughter comes home from school and tells you about the new kid in class with the northern accent.

"Ah whander how come people from uup Nawth tawk sooo funny," she said to me.

I've noticed that in the past few years both my daughters have started stretching one-syllable words into two syllables. But I drew the line one night when my older daughter said, "would yawl pass the sawt and peppuh?"

Speech patterns aren't the only way you can tell if a Yankee has been in the South too long. How else can you tell? Well, you know you've been in Florida too long if:

● You call cockroaches "palmetto bugs."

● You stand your ground when you see a palmetto bug, rather than running for the bed.

● You uproot the oleander to make room for more aloe plants.

● You don't call the police to report a plane crash every time you see a mosquito plane spraying your neighborhood.

● You don't go in the Gulf because you've seen the creatures that come out of the Gulf.

● Your kids refer to the pile of dirt in the lot next door as "the mountain."

● You know that the driver in front of you is going to turn left when his right turn signal is blinking.

- Your daughter looks like Kermit the frog because the chlorine in the pool has turned her hair green.
- Despite the color of your daughter's hair, you know that the water in the swimming pool is constantly on the verge of turning brown.
- You think of a hurricane as just another storm to interrupt the weekend.
- Your kid wants a boat for his 10th birthday.
- You stop looking on the yard as decorative landscaping and start referring to it as "the enemy."
- You encourage little green lizzards to take up residence with you because they're preferable to the bugs.
- You refer to anything built earlier than 1960 as "antique."
- You complain about the cold weather every time the thermometer dips below 60 degrees.

You may be asking yourself, "How does she know these things?" Well, I've lived in Florida for more than five years, and that just about makes me a semi-native.

For a lot of you that may not seem like much of an accomplishment. But you've got to understand, before we moved here my husband promised me that if I didn't love the sunshine state at the end of two years, we could head back north.

I'll never forget my first day in Florida. I stepped off the airplane, felt the humidity, and said "We can't live here! I've got naturally curly hair!"

My life has been one big frizzball ever since.

I'd like to say that during the first two years my blood thinned out, I became less terrified of roaches, I stopped worrying about skin cancer, I got used to turning on the cold faucet and receiving warm water, and I didn't miss the leaves changing colors in the fall. Well, actually, I did start to like the place a bit.

"Maybe we should give it another year," I said to my husband on our second anniversary in Florida. Of course I knew that if I insisted on moving back north, I would be

17

moving by myself. He had no intention of leaving his little slice of paradise.

Over the years I've learned a lot about life in the sunshine.

For instance, no matter how inviting a swimming pool looks in February, you are risking cardiac arrest by taking a quick plunge. If you survive, you haven't been here long enough.

If there's a traffic jam, it must be raining. Have you ever noticed how all traffic slows to a snail's pace even in the lightest of rain showers?

If they're fixing a road, it must be the tourist season. When rain doesn't cause traffic jams, road construction does. And for some reason most road construction projects are started just about the time the first snowbird arrives for winter.

I've learned that limes still cost 65 cents each, even if there is a tree full of them in the lot next to the supermarket. But one lemon tree is enough to supply the entire neighborhood.

If the roach is considered the state insect, then surely the state pet must be the love bug, which greets carloads of tourists on their way down through Florida each year. Just think how many happy visitors go home with a little, "I Lovebug Florida" on their front bumper.

And that's how a semi-native sees it.

6
Chum upon the waters

Just when you thought it was safe to go to the refrigerator again, along comes **CHUM.**

Fast on the heels of Jaws II and Jaws 3-D, CHUM is stirring up local waters. Is it a movie? Is it a new organic food?

Until last month I though chum was someone you would take fishing with you. Even though avid fishermen don't go out for an afternoon of conversation, I figured it would be nice to have a chum aboard to help pass the time.

But then I found out what chum really is . . . and all I can say is **G-R-O-S-S!**

Chum, for those of you who aren't up on all those fancy terms that fishermen use, is a disgusting mixture of ground up blood and guts. You toss it into the water to attract sharks.

Why, you might ask, would anyone in their right mind try to attract sharks? Well, you might want a few around if you were making a movie. Or you might want some to scare off swimmers if you planned to go skinny dipping. But I've been tossing chum upon the waters to get dinner.

Shark, it seems, is delicious to eat. Kind of ironic, isn't it? After all these years of sharks eating people, the tables are turned and people are now eating shark.

To catch a shark, though, you first have to attract him to your boat. And that's where chum comes in handy.

You can buy a box of dried chum and sprinkle it on the

water like you would throw soap flakes into a washing machine. Or you can sink a milk container full of dried chum in the water, punch a few holes in the container and let the chum ooze out slowly.

But the best kind of chum comes frozen. It's kind of like buying a box of frozen peas. You rip off the container, throw the frozen block of chum in a net bag, toss it in the water and wait for the sharks to come calling.

The first time I opened the frozen chum, I peeled off the cardboard box and found an eyeball staring up at me.

"What is this stuff?" I asked my husband.

"Ground up fish," he said casually.

"Well, they didn't grind it enough," I told him, tossing the chum over the side of the boat as quickly as possible.

As in life, good chum is hard to find.

I know a man who brings home the catfish he catches. He stuffs them in his wife's Cuisinart, grinds them up and makes his own chum. If I were his wife, I don't know which would be the first to go . . . the Cuisinart or the husband. We certainly would not be on chummy terms.

Our chum comes from a little bait shop on Sanibel that makes the finest concoction around. In fact I would call it gourmet chum, especially considering the price.

I usually buy half a dozen bags of frozen chum at a time, just to save the trip over the bridge each time I want to go fishing. But what do you do with six boxes of frozen chum?

You guessed it. Our freezer is now chock-full of chum. That presents a problem, however. You can just imagine what ground up blood and guts smells like as it defrosts. And that's exactly what the inside of my freezer smells like.

For weeks, everything that came out of my refrigerator smelled like dead fish. The ice cubes made a drink undrinkable. The ground beef tasted like snapper. The fruit had a smell all its own.

While I've never been known for a sparkling clean re-

frigerator, my reputation sank to a new low. My kids wouldn't even walk through the kitchen. They claimed the odor was seeping through the cracks of the freezer and stinking up the whole room. My neighbor asked if we had switched exterminators. The animals on our street started to gather at our front door.

I found plastic garbage bags to be the solution. If you wrap each box of chum in 20 of those extra-thick garbage bags, the smell is somewhat retarded. Of course there isn't room for anything else, but that's no problem . . . shark is on its way.

You'd be amazed at how fast chum attracts sharks. In no time at all you'll see fins circling your boat, heading for your chum bag. I don't mind telling you, it can be a little unnerving.

Sharks like to eat your line as well as your bait. They can snap a leader faster than you can say "jaws." But a little patience is all that's needed.

Sooner or later a dumb shark will swim by and actually get hooked. That's when the fight begins. The real trick in shark fishing is getting the shark to swim into your net. After that, it's all over.

Once you get a shark out of the water, you club him senseless with a billy club. After all, who wants to have anything with a set of teeth like that aboard your boat? Only a dentist!

My daughter couldn't believe the sight of her father clubbing the first shark. She cried, comparing it with the clubbing of the baby seals. When he cut off the head and tossed it into the chum bag, she vowed to stay home the next trip.

The end result was heavenly. As we were enjoying our first shark cooked on the grill last month, my husband started adding up the cost.

"Let's see. The new fishing rod was $79, and the chum cost $18. The gas and oil for the boat came to $24, and the bait was $8. The net was $8.50 and the knife came to $12. That means this shark cost us about $50 a pound."

I guess the shark did have the last bite after all!

7
If this is paradise, why am I sweating?

The Chamber of Commerce might never admit it, but there's trouble down here in paradise!

It's not the 100 degree temperatures that make your clothes so wet they look like they just came out of the washing machine.

It's not the "no-see-ums" that attack any area of your skin left untouched by mosquitoes.

It's not the humidity that can turn your lovely new coif into a frizzy, unruly mop in just five minutes.

Nope. I'm talking about something that puts terror in the hearts of every Florida homeowner . . . that causes housewives to bite their fingernails down to the quick and has reduced grown men to tears.

Folks, I mean THE ELECTRIC BILL!!!

That little envelope that arrives every month from the electric company has been the cause of more than one divorce, I'm sure.

I can always tell when the first electric bill of the summer has been delivered at our house. My husband flings open the windows, shuts off the air conditioner and shouts in his most convincing voice, "Feel this cool breeze!"

Last summer was different. I went through the mail every day, trying to head off trouble. When the bill arrived, I held it back, waiting for a day when he was in a better mood.

When I finally did present the electric bill to him, he nearly went into cardiac arrest. And when I picked the bill off the floor, I saw why.

"This can't be right," I told him between breaths as I tried to revive him with CPR. "There's got to be some mistake."

After a few phone calls to friends and relatives, I found out there was no mistake. We owed the electric company every penny of the amount.

In fact, the electric company told me that the next bill would probably be higher, since it was a hotter month. That's just great!

So my husband came up with some energy-saving ideas of his own . . . things we can do to use less electricity and save money.

He decided one big electric expense is the filter system for our swimming pool. If we shut off the filter system, we could save lots of money, he claims.

"You'll just have to stop thinking of it as a pool, and start thinking of it as a little lake," he told the kids.

"When the water turns green and the scum starts to form on the top, we can stock it with fish," he said. "You can walk out the door and catch your own dinner."

And it doesn't end there.

"We can sell our boat and buy one of those little inflatable boats to use on our little lake," he said. "Just think of the gas money we'd save!"

There were other ideas, too. He said that since the air conditioner used most of the electricity, we could learn to get along without it. Just open all the windows at night, and keep them closed during the day, he said.

"That's fine for you," I told him. "You're in an air-conditioned office all day. You don't have to spend the day locked in a hot box with two sweaty kids."

Of course he had a solution.

25

"Get out of the house," he said. "Spend the day in the supermarket. You spend so much time and money there every week that it's already like your second home."

He had other suggestions that were equally ridiculous.

"Keep the clothes in the refrigerator," he told me. "That will cool you off during the day."

"And wear roller skates while you're doing the housework. That way you'll always have a breeze."

I told him it was impossible to get by this summer without air conditioning, no matter what price we had to pay.

"Well, in that case we will have to cut back on something else," he said. "No lights will be used until the cooler weather starts. And no more warm showers. It's cool baths from now on."

My older daughter found it a little hard to accept the news that she couldn't use her hair drier anymore.

"This is Florida," my husband told her. "You don't use blow driers in Florida!"

26

After days of arguing about energy-saving ideas, I offered what I considered the only possible solution to high electric bills.

"Why don't I take the kids to the mountains for two months every summer," I said. "You can stay here in the your un-air conditioned splendor and save money."

He thought that sounded like a good idea, which came as a surprise to me. But then came the kicker.

"We can't afford it. We owe the electric company too much money."

Things can only get hotter!

8
Deck the pool
with boughs of folly

Surely one of the biggest problems of living in Florida must be what to do with your stocking at Christmas.

I mean just how many fireplaces have you seen since you moved south?

Just last December I had a friend from New York visiting with us, and we were talking about the different lifestyle in Florida.

"Well, where do you hang your stockings?" she asked me one night at the dinner table.

"On the shower curtain rod," I replied.

"That's a strange place," she said.

"Well where do you hang **your** stockings?" I asked her.

"On the fireplace," she said.

"Now **that's** a strange place," I told her.

It took us a few more minutes of strange conversation to realize that she was talking about Christmas stockings and I was talking about pantyhose.

That just underlines the dilemma I face each year when the kids start wondering how Santa Claus is going to get into our house, and whether he will ever discover our stockings.

During our first year in Florida, Santa found the Christmas stockings hanging from the dials on the stereo in the living room. It seemed a bit strange, but they did the trick.

Another year we decided that the handles on the drawer of one of the end tables would make a dandy substitute fireplace, but the loaded stockings nearly tipped the table over.

In other years we have tried door handles, desk drawers, chair arms and bed posts. But I haven't gone so far as my friend.

Her children got fed up with the annual problem, so one year they got a large sheet of paper, drew a fireplace on it and hung it on the door. Then they tacked their stockings to the "fireplace" and went to bed happy. Naturally, Santa rewards ingenuity.

The stocking isn't the only problem in Florida. My little daughter has asked me at least 25 times how Santa Claus can get into the house when there's no chimney. Somehow, "he walks in the front door" takes away a lot of the excitement and mystery of Christmas.

"But how does his sleigh work if there's no snow?"

Would you believe a helicopter?

"But where will the reindeer be?"

Maybe they don't go south of North Carolina.

"But what will happen to Rudolph?"

Who needs a spotlight in this clear sky?

"But what if his helicopter breaks?"

There's always the Coast Guard.

"Does he ever come by boat?"

Why not? I guess if you can decorate palm trees with twinkle lights, Santa Claus can come by boat.

Actually, these problems loom big in my daughter's mind, but as long as Santa delivers on Christmas morning, he can take any kind of transportation he wants.

9
The great escape

Every year I spend the last two weeks of May frantically searching for the right summer camp—for myself.

The thought of spending three months locked in an air-conditioned house with two children and a dog is giving me Excedrin Headache No. 497.

The first few days of summer are never too bad. But by day three, when the boredom sets in and the kids are trying to teach the dog to fetch the stick that's in the neighbor's yard on the other side of the canal, you know it's time to fill their lives with some organized activity. That's activity organized by someone else!

As much as I'd like to purchase a large trunk and pack my kids off to some camp in the mountains, I keep having these visions of some camp counselor using my little girl's arm for a marshmallow-roasting stick. Not that I haven't thought of that myself on a bad day.

And of course there is the financial problem. A lot of those far-away camps have a price tag that looks more like the first-year tuition at Yale than two months at a summer camp. And what mother with one child facing braces and another child begging for a new bike can afford to blow that big a wad, no matter how much relief is at stake.

So I stopped sewing the name tags in the size 8 underwear and started looking for a day camp that had bus service.

Frankly, I've always had good luck with the local day camps. My older daughter came home a few times with a greenish cast because she was afraid to use the outdoor bathrooms, but if she can hold it from 9 a.m. to 3 p.m., I figure that's just another learning experience.

As I was signing the kids up last year, however, I suddenly realized that summer camp is wasted on children. I don't know a mother who wouldn't sell her soul for a few weeks at camp . . . without the kids!

Just imagine sitting around a campfire and not worrying about what time the sitter has to be home. Or whether the dog's germs will ever come out of the toothbrush. Or whether the lizard in the washing machine will soil all the clothes or just the pocket of the jeans it was living in.

Camp food may taste yucky to the kids, but what mother in her right mind is going to turn her nose up at a meal that is cooked by someone else? And served to her by someone else? And she wouldn't even have to worry about the dishes!

There's another factor. Can you imagine the ecstacy of not having to tackle that three o'clock question of "What's for dinner?" every afternoon. The way I see it, the biggest decision of the day would be whether to go fishing or swimming.

Sure, there might be problems.

I personally wouldn't want to waste an afternoon learning how to tie 58 different types of knots. Unless, of course, they could be used on the kids at some future time.

And the thought of living for more than three days without access to a washing machine makes me a little nervous.

There's also the matter of eight middle-aged women crowded into one little cabin for a week or two. Where do they plug in the curling irons? Will there be enough L'Oreal to go around? Who gets to use the 12-inch-by-18-inch mirror first? Will anyone remember how to short-sheet a bed? How can they call home without a telephone by the bed?

I guess sending mothers to camp isn't such a hot idea after all.

10

What's so great about dawn's early light?

There's an old Flemish proverb that says "He who laughs last laughs longest, but he who sleepeth longest deserves ridicule."

You don't hear much about the old Flems these days, but their wisdom endures.

There are two types of people in this world: night people and morning people.

Night people like to stay up late and enjoy life to the fullest. Generally, they're fun to be around. Morning people like to get up before the sun rises and brag about how much they accomplish. Generally, they're insufferable bores.

For some unexplainable reason, night people always marry morning people and are subject to relentless criticism for the rest of their married life.

Children are praised for taking naps. Dogs can lay around all day and nobody kicks them. But let an adult try to sleep in late and the world collapses.

For nine months of the year I get up at the crack of dawn, pack lunch boxes, and do my best to greet the world with a smile.

And every morning, as I spread another load of peanut butter across another slice of bread, I murmer to myself, "48 more days before school's out; 47 more days until I

get to sleep in; 46 days until school is out; 45 more days . . ."

But it just wasn't in the cards this year.

On the first Monday after school ended, my husband shook me awake frantically. "You better get up quick," he said. "The kids are going to be late for school."

I lifted one eyelid with my index finger, squinted out at the clock, saw the little hand pointing to 7, reached over, grabbed the clock and threw it at him.

On Tuesday morning I heard screams coming from the family room. I staggered out of bed at 5 a.m. and found the kids fighting over which test pattern they were going to watch on the television set.

I ripped the TV cord out of the wall, tore the TV Guide into little pieces, and yelled **"GET BACK IN YOUR BEDS!"** I tried to catch a few more winks of sleep, but I heard some heavy sobbing and felt a tear running down my forehead. I opened my eyes and found my younger daughter standing at my side, weeping, "Now I'll never get to see Mr. Rogers again."

On Wednesday the phone rang at 8:15 a.m. It was my friend Nelda.

"Did I wake you up?" she asked cautiously. For some strange reason I tried to hide the fact that I was in the middle of a deep sleep.

"No," I assured her. "My voice always sounds like this before sunrise. It's just a little post-nasal drip. One cup of coffee will wash it away."

Thursday was a little better. I made it all the way to 8:45 before the doorbell rang. I groped my way to the front door, opened it and stood face-to-face with the exterminator, who was making his monthly house call.

"A little bug spray will take the cobwebs out of your eyes," he joked. "Or do you want me to come back a little later when you're among the living?"

He wasn't laughing after I wrapped the hose of his bug sprayer around his neck and started hitting him over the head with a rat trap. I know I'm no beauty when I just wake up, but making fun of a customer is going a bit too far.

On Friday morning the phone rang at 8:30 and a man on the other end of the line tried to sell me a cemetery plot. I had just drifted back to sleep when there was a knock on the door from a little kid selling magazine subscriptions. I propped my head on the pillow and was ready to doze off again when the phone started ringing off the hook. My college was having a telethon to raise money for a new building. I pledged my alarm clock.

The next morning I woke up with a tiny foot sticking in my shoulder. The sun was just coming up, and in the dim light of morning I saw both kids sharing my bed. The dog was there, too.

True, they were all sleeping. That's the good news. The bad news is there wasn't any room left for me in the bed. So I resigned myself to another early day.

Sooner or later the world's going to succeed in making me a morning person, too.

11
Sex and the 6-year-old

Kids today know a lot more than I did when I was that age.

My 11-year-old daughter asks questions I never thought of asking until I was in high school. And even then I was too embarrassed to ask them.

I blame it for the most part on television. Just the other night I found the kids watching a practically nude Bo Derek cavorting with Tarzan (who would have been covered up more by a fig leaf than the loin cloth he was wearing) and a rather forward-thinking monkey.

Yes, with all those scantily clad people running across the television screen every day, it doesn't leave much to the imagination. But it's more than television. Everywhere the kids look, everyone they talk to, they're getting information that was previously "classified."

My husband is still shaking his head about my daughter's request to go see that new movie starring Burt Reynolds and Dolly Parton. "It's about a warehouse in Texas," she said.

Where do you go from there?

Actually, nothing the kids say shocks me any more. Just the other day I was bringing a group of 6-year-olds home from day camp, and one little girl obviously had a story to tell.

"I'd tell you about what happened with my cousin this

summer but I'd be too embarrassed," she said quietly in my ear.

I assured her that she didn't have to tell if it would embarrass her. But she would not be put off.

"I told my brother, and he always teases me," she said, with a little more assurance. "That's why I can't tell you."

"No problem," I told her. "Forget the whole subject."

"Yeah, it's too embarrassing, or I'd tell you," the 6-year-old girl said.

By this time it had finally sunk in that she clearly had a good story to tell, and she was just waiting for the audience to beg. So I went after the bait.

"What happened with your cousin this summer," I asked trying to conceal the smile.

"Well, since you asked, my cousin and I did something and now my brother is always making fun of me."

Another childhood rivalry, I thought to myself.

"Well just what did you and your cousin do," I asked her, with visions of picking blueberries and running through a field of daisies in my mind.

"It's what you do after you get married," she said.

I wasn't ready for that! Talk about a bad reaction . . . I nearly wrecked the car. The best way to drop this whole discussion is to change the subject, I decided.

"What happened at camp today," I asked, hoping someone else would talk about something else. But the little girl would not be put off by any diversionary tactics.

"You know what you do after you get married," she said to me.

"Noooo, I don't." My mind was racing, trying desperately to come up with some conclusion other than the obvious one.

"Sure you do. What did you and your husband do after you got married?" she said.

"Ummmmm . . . we went to a reception," I said in a low voice, hoping to somehow exclude the other little kids from this conversation as it headed in the wrong direction.

"No," she said, clearly annoyed. "What did you do?"

"Well, we cut the cake."

"No! Not that. What did you do after that?"

"We danced," I said, more of a question than a statement, hoping that this cat-and-mouse game would soon end.

"Noooo! You know, what does a bride do?"

"She tosses her bouquet."

"No, no, no. What did you and your husband do after that?"

"We went to Bermuda." I was quickly coming to the end, and I dreaded the next question.

The little girl looked at me in disbelief. "Didn't you and your husband kiss?"

Wow! What a relief!

"Oh, sure. Yeah, we kissed. Right. We kissed. Just after we got married. You're right. How could I forget. We kissed."

"Well that's what my cousin and I did, and now my brother laughs at me," she said, not really understanding the sudden relief I felt.

I guess what Art Linkletter said is true. Kids do say the darnedest things, but adults give them credit for a lot more than they really deserve.

12
Love at first byte

English is on its way out. A whole new language is taking over in Florida, and it's not Spanish. I'm talking about "computer language."

As millions of Americans plug into home computers, talk at cocktail parties no longer centers on the stock market or tax-saving tips. Instead, conversation revolves around microchips and word processing.

"I hear IBM is coming out with a new 128K compatible double density disk drive with 250,000 bits per second and on-board software."

"You're kidding! Will it have a graphics plotter and an appropriate user bus?"

"No, but it is capable of a 25-line-by-80-character display, with a 40-80 character switch. I'm thinking about getting one for the kids."

Everywhere you go, people are talking about software and component boards like they were apples—I mean oranges. Even in K-Mart, where you'd expect to find customers haggling over which case of motor oil to buy, you see people pushing carts down the aisles comparing the features of the Atari 800 and the Commodore 64.

There's no use hiding from reality. In 10 years we'll all be interfacing with each other instead of conversing.

Until recently, I didn't know what a "megabyte" was.

I was oblivious to things like microprocessors, floppy disks and matrix variables.

I thought software was a new kind of rubber table setting for children. If someone asked me about peripherals, I assumed they were talking about contact lenses.

I took it for granted that 64K was a better grade of gold, and the only chips I knew anything about were poker chips. In other words, computers were not compatible with my memory.

When my daughter came home from school last year talking about the apple she worked on in class, it took me days to figure out she was talking about a computer. I just assumed they were teaching her some biology. Little did I dream they were programming her to be a part of the computer generation.

I later discovered, however, that once you put an 11-year-old in front of a computer screen for one hour, she will eventually drive everyone else in the family crazy with outrageous reasons for why she needs her own personal computer. And of course what parent wants to be responsible for her child being left behind in the race for that new high-tech life we've been told to expect?

Once you start to poke around the computer stores, you quickly come to the realization that no family in America can really afford to live without its own personal computer. These marvelous machines organize the family budget, help you with the household inventory, keep your appointment schedule, and even plug you into information sources.

"If we had a computer, I could balance my checkbook," I told my husband, trying to get him interested.

"I seriously doubt that you could ever balance your checkbook," he shot back. "You haven't kept a check stub for 15 years, and I don't think you're about to start now. Besides, if we bought a computer, my checkbook wouldn't balance for the next six months."

I knew I wasn't getting anywhere.

"I could put all my recipes on the computer, and then I wouldn't have to hunt all over the kitchen for the recipe I want."

"I'd like to see you typing all those recipes. Besides, you already know the recipe for tuna noodle casserole by heart, and that's about all you cook anymore."

Despite his resistence, I knew he was interested. How else did all those computer sales brochures get in our house?

Buying a computer is a lot like buying stock. After you've finally decided on which one to buy, you never know when to buy it because the price is certain to be different tomorrow.

Since computer prices are dropping faster than roller coasters, there's always the fear that your neighbor will go out on Wednesday and pay $199 for the same computer you purchased on Tuesday for $299. Nobody likes to feel that foolish!

"The way they're slashing these prices every week, we could wait until December, when they're sure to be giving them away in Cracker Jack boxes," my husband suggested.

I spent one entire week on the phone comparing prices, and the very day we decided to buy our own home computer, the family TV set had a fatal heart attack. By this time we were so caught up in the computer frenzy that another $250 for a television set didn't seem unreasonable.

The computer has been sitting on our bedroom floor for weeks, hooked up to our new TV set by some sort of magical lifeline. My daughter is the only person in our family who can interface with it.

You see, the computer speaks several different languages, but I don't understand any of them. If not English, I was kind of hoping for fluent French. Instead, I got BASIC. And Pascal. And Logo. Have you ever tried to conduct a conversation in Pascal?

"What is this BASIC I've been reading about in this crazy instruction manual?" I asked the salesman on my third trip back after buying the computer.

"BASIC is the language the computer speaks," he told me.

"Why doesn't it speak English?"

"It can't understand English. It can only understand machine language," he said.

"Well, if this machine was as smart as you told me it was, it could learn how to understand English." I guess I shot down one more myth about computers.

Even though I'm having a hard time adjusting to the culture shock of dealing with another language in our house, our kids seem to be able to grasp computer language better than they can understand their Spanish lessons.

My daughter brought home a computer magazine last week. I can only compare it with the tax tables the Internal Revenue Service publishes each year. If you get your kicks from looking at columns of numbers and strange symbols, then you should definitely get a subscription. There isn't a complete sentence in the entire issue.

"Look at this new 128K compatible double density disk drive with 250,000 bits per second and on-board software," my daughter said, showing me a page from her computer magazine. I guess it could be worse. She could have become a Valley Girl!

As for me, I know that by pushing a few keys on our new computer, I can type my name in colored letters on the TV screen, but I'm really more confused than ever. Microprocessors and peripherals are still just mysteries.

But I do know what a megabyte is. It's a word that refers to amounts or values. An example of how the word is used can be seen in this sentence: "Our new home computer took a **megabyte** out of our checking account."

Sometimes you have to spend a lot to learn a little!

13
Reality can be the quiche of death

When two people tell me they're living together before getting married so they will be sure they're compatible, I just laugh.

Not that I have anything against them living together. It's the compatibility test that's such a joke.

If a couple really wants to test their relationship, they should share their apartment with a sick toddler who has a tendency to throw up in the middle of the night, a teen-ager with a telephone receiver growing out of her right ear, a three-year-old "puppy" that is nearly house-trained, and a 10-year-old refrigerator with an icemaker that goes "kachunck, kachunck, kachunck" all night long.

If the two are still together at the end of a month, they are compatible.

Premarital bliss is breakfast in bed; linen napkins; candlelight and soft music. Reality is a little kid waking you up at 6 a.m. waving a soggy diaper in your face; paper napkins and plastic spoons; and candlelight only when there is a power failure.

If two young lovebirds think compatibility is learning to share the same tube of toothpaste, they are wasting a lot of valuable time.

While it's true that toothpaste is the foundation of a good relationship, it goes a lot further than simply sharing.

In real life, finding the toothpaste is the challenge. And when it turns up, there is often a ring of dog hair around the sticky end of the tube. If you can wipe off the dog hair and use the toothpaste without letting loose with a string of accusations, then you are learning to be compatible.

Going to the grocery store together might seem like a fun experience for two naive young people in love. My advice is to take the neighbor's three little kids along and then tell me about fun.

If you are still speaking to each other after one kid knocks down a display of applesauce jars, another kid opens up a box of detergent and spreads soap powder all over the floor, and the third rolls cans of tomatoes down the aisles like bowling balls, then you might make it. If one of you ends up sitting in the car for an hour reading Sports Illustrated, however, I wouldn't be too anxious to invest in any monogrammed sheets.

I guess it all boils down to the fact that if a man and woman are going to test their compatibility by living together, there should be a few kids around to help them grade the exam.

For example, every women knows what kind of reaction she gets when she caresses a man. But before she gets married she should know what the man's reaction will be when a baby throws up all over his new blue blazer. Just remember, marriage involves a lot of caressing, but it also involves a lot of throwing up.

It might be a good idea for the woman to spend all day Saturday washing the kitchen floor, cleaning the toilet bowls, and defrosting the freezer while the man spends the day on the sofa watching football games. If she can still sit down at the dinner table that night and be cheerful, I'd feel she has a better grasp of reality. Just ignore those television commercials that show two people enjoying a sunny afternoon on a sailboat.

There are a variety of tests you can take to explore compatibility.

HIS HERS

Accidentally knock over a glass of milk during dinner and see what happens. Will he make any attempt to mop it up? Which goes away first—the smell in the carpet or the blame he is holding over your head?

Send him to the grocery store with a $20 bill and see what he comes home with. Sardines, pepperoni, roquefort cheese, fishing hooks, and a paint-by-numbers kit? Or steak, lima beans, bean sprouts, yogurt and window cleaner.

Let the bathroom water faucet drip and see how long it takes him to notice. After he notices, see how long it takes him to get around to fixing it. Be sure to ask him if he thinks you should call a plumber!

The ultimate test of compatibility is wallpaper. Not choosing it, but hanging it. If the two of you can wallpaper the bathroom together, then I'd suggest marriage. You've at least got a fighting chance.

14

These are the times
that try moms' souls

The older kids get, the tougher it is to make a family decision.

Trying to arrange a vacation, for example, is like putting together a worldwide economic summit meeting.

One kid can't go away **until** August because she's enrolled in summer camp. The other can't go away **in** August because that's when the computer class starts. Of course she could take the computer class in July, but then she'd miss gymnastics. "And besides, we can't go away in August because that's when the school's bunny rabbit comes to stay with us," my daughter informed me. "Everyone is taking turns, and my turn is August."

If, by some fluke, you can find a week to accommodate everyone, trying to decide where to go is enough to kill the whole vacation before it even starts. My family hasn't been able to agree on a destination for years.

But the big decisions aren't the real problem. Little decisions are the killer.

Take toothpaste, for instance. If I buy Crest, the kids complain because it isn't Colgate. If I buy gel, they squeeze it out of the tube and say "Yuk! This is gross!" If there is only red and white striped toothpaste, they ask me where the mint-flavored tube is. It's enough to make you beg them not to brush their teeth.

Another decision-making problem involves television. We have two television sets and four people in our house, but clearly that's not enough. TV sets, that is!

One child never gets out of arm's length from the channel selector knob, flipping it every 30 seconds to see if there is anything better on another channel. Take my word, it is somewhat disconcerting.

The other child will never watch what her sister is watching on TV, as a matter of principle. That leads to constant arguing, usually at a volume louder than the television set. When she actually wants to watch the same show as her sister, she goes into the other room and turns the same channel on, too proud to admit that she might be interested in the same thing her sister likes.

But the toughest decision facing any family today is what kind of pizza to order.

We went to a pizza restaurant recently, sat down, and scanned the selections.

"I want mushrooms and pepperoni."

"I don't want pepperoni. I want sausage."

"Don't put any sausage on mine. I just want cheese."

"I changed my mind. Make it cheese and olives, but no sausage."

"Why don't we try olives and onions and bacon?"

"Nobody likes onions."

"I do!"

"Gross!"

"How about a pizza with everything on it?"

"I hate anchovies."

"Be quiet. Here comes the waitress."

"Have you decided?"

"Yes. We want a medium piz . . ."

"Make it large. Everyone's hungry."

"We want a large pizza with mushrooms and sausage and . . ."

"No! Leave off the sausage."

"But I want sausage!"

49

"We want a large pizza with mushrooms on half of it and bacon on a quarter of it and olives . . ."

"WAIT! I changed my mind about the sausage."

"And I want extra cheese but no olives."

"Could you come back in five minutes? We haven't reached a decision yet."

After five more minutes of arguing, my husband stood up and headed for the door.

"Where are you going?" the kids yelled across the restaurant.

"To a fast food place where there aren't so many decisions to make," he said as he walked out the door.

"Let's go to McDonalds," one kid said in the car.

"No, I want to go to Burger King," the other one said.

I've decided that you just can't win!

15
You can't win for losing

Let's face it, there are some things in life that you just can't win—the Publisher's Clearing House Sweepstakes; a battle with the Internal Revenue Service; an argument with an 11-year-old.

Have you ever known any adult who has come out on top after a knock-down drag-out argument with a kid? Be honest, now!

No matter what the subject, and no matter who initiates it, when an adult is reduced to arguing with an 11-year-old, the kid will win every time.

This isn't something I learned in Child Psychology 101. This is from first-hand experience.

Bedtime is a good example.

After dinner at our house, the adults and the children both get keyed up for the big battle. And every night, at 8:30, the bugle sounds and the joust begins.

"It's time for bed," I say.

Suddenly everyone has lost their hearing.

"It's time to get ready for bed," I say a little louder.

"Aw, mom! Can't I stay up and see the next show?"

"No, it's bedtime."

"But mom," my daughter says, searching desperately to find the TV Guide. "There's a really great show on now. Please!"

"No, get to bed."

Now many people, seeing the kid head for the bedroom, might think the battle has been won by mother. But those people obviously never had kids!

"Mother," she says 15 minutes later, "I can't find my pajamas."

Score two points for the kid. If I tell her to find them herself, it means another 15-minute delay before bedtime. But if I go in to her bedroom and find the pajamas myself, it means she has me trained to do her work for her. Either way, she wins.

"You had them on last," I tell her. "You find them yourself."

That's clearly the better response. So 15 agonizing minutes later, she steps out of her bedroom and heads for the TV Guide.

"Did you brush your teeth?" I ask her.

"I'm waiting until after I have dessert," she says.

"You had dessert after dinner. Now brush your teeth."

That's a minor victory for me, but of course she had the last say.

"Mom, I can't find my toothbrush. Have you seen it?"

If I ignore her, she will go to bed with dirty teeth and you know what that means—cavities, receding gums, root canals, dentures, and dental bills that will rival the national debt.

There it is. I can find her toothbrush and save her from all that agony, or I can ignore it and pay the dental bills in five years. So score two more points for the kid.

After the teeth are nice and clean, it's time for bed, right?

"I forgot to kiss dad," she says, getting out of bed and waltzing into the living room. A quick kiss for dad, a kiss for the dog, a hug for dad, a hug for the dog, another kiss for dad, another kiss for . . .

Five minutes later, she has meandered through the house and finally found her way to bed. "Can I read before I go to sleep?"

Of course no mother in her right mind would say no to that question.

"You can read for ten minutes, and then you've got to turn the light out."

Ten minutes later I turn off my stop-watch and announce, "bedtime."

"I'll turn the light off as soon as I finish reading this chapter," she says.

Five minutes later, "bedtime."

"Just one more sentence to go on this page!"

Five minutes later, "bedtime."

"Alright," she says, slamming the book closed.

When the lights go out, you would score a victory for mother, right? Wrong!

"I forgot to get a glass of water."

Ignore it.

"Mother! I forgot to get a glass of water!"

Ignore it again.

"Can I please get a glass of water?"

"No."

"But I'm dying of thirst! I've got to have water!"

Sure enough, she wins another victory.

"Get your water and get right back in bed," I yell.

"She runs to the kitchen, gets a glass, fills it with ice, runs to the sink, fills it with water, and then suddenly she goes into slow motion.

She strolls through the family room, stopping at the table to study the flowers in the vase. She puts down the glass of water and walks her fingers across the table top, picking up a ceramic ashtray.

"What's this?" she says, holding the ashtray up in the air, turning it from side to side as if she's never seen an ashtray before.

"Put that down and **GET TO BED!**"

"**OKAY, OKAY!!!** I'm going!"

At last she's in bed. I sit down, weary from another night of battle, thinking I've only got a few more years to go.

"Mother . . . you forgot to kiss me good night!"

I knew it. She won again. I guess I'm just outmatched.

16

For whom the bell tolls . . . always for me!

I'm the victim of telephone tyranny.

For some unexplainable reason, the telephone has a terrible hold over me. When it rings, I have to answer it.

If I'm in the shower and the phone rings, I grab a towel and run to answer it. I usually spend five minutes standing in a puddle of water, shivering while I listen to somebody trying to sell me a magazine subscription.

If I'm getting out of the car with an armful of groceries and I hear the phone ringing, I drop the bags and fumble with the key to the house so I can race in and grab the phone before it stops ringing.

If the telephone bell jogs me out of a deep sleep at 6 in the morning, I stumble out of bed, answer the phone and try to assure the caller that, "Heavens no, the phone didn't wake me up. I've been up for hours. My voice sounds like this because I've got a bad cold."

I guess I feel compelled to answer the telephone because I'm always curious about who is on the other end of the line. I can't stand the suspense of letting the phone ring and not knowing who wants to talk with me.

My husband, on the other hand, claims that I've become a slave to the telephone.

"You respond to the telephone without thinking about whether it is serving you or you are serving it," he says.

That's easy for him to say. He never even hears the telephone ring. Or at least he pretends he doesn't.

Let's say he's standing in the kitchen, at arm's length from the phone, and I'm in the bathroom, three rooms away from the nearest extension. And the telephone starts to ring. Guess who ends up answering it?

I admit it's a little thing, but that doesn't mean it isn't annoying.

"Why don't you answer it?" I said one day as the phone was jangling off the hook.

"Why should I answer it?" he shot back. "The phone is never for me!"

"How do you know unless you answer it?"

"I know."

"But I'm busy fixing dinner."

"But you're closer."

"My hands are all greasy."

"Get a paper towel."

I couldn't stand it any longer. I picked up the phone, just in time to hear a click.

"Now I'll never know who it was," I said, glaring at him.

"They'll call back," he said, completely unperturbed.

They did, 15 minutes later, just as I was sitting down at the dinner table. And no, I didn't buy the magazine subscriptions they were selling. I just hung up.

17
Don't say "I do" until you pop the question

Some subjects just shouldn't be discussed.

But I feel it's my duty to issue a warning to all those women who have recently found true love and are considering a trip to the altar.

The biggest mystery in marriage doesn't involve sex, or money, or love. No, it involves toilet paper.

If your sweetheart proposes, my suggestion to you is to ask him one simple question before you say yes. Confront him point blank: "Do you know how to replace an empty roll of toilet paper?"

Sure, it's an awkward topic for such a tender moment. But if you don't ask him then, you'll regret it the rest of your life.

Chances are, your true love will be noncomittal. He'll try to avoid an answer.

Don't be fooled. Demand a direct response. After all, it's your right to know.

If his answer is "yes," get it in writing. Don't be carried away by the moment. Make sure his promise is down there in black and white. Check to see if he has used disappearing ink, too. You can never be too careful, you know!

If his answer is "no," dump him and search for another mate. Honesty is a great quality in a man, but after 40 years of being the only person in the house who knows how to change a roll of toilet paper, honesty grows a bit thin on the quality scale.

After you dump him, start searching for Mr. Right immediately. I estimate there are only a few dozen men in the country who can change a roll of toilet paper, and they're in big demand. Most of them are already taken, as a matter of fact.

So you and 500,000 other women are all looking for the same man who holds the all-important knowledge. The battle will be fierce.

You're probably asking yourself, "How does she know so much about this strange topic?"

Simple! I've been married 15 years, and in all that time my husband hasn't once changed a roll of toilet paper.

"Surely the children will help," you're probably saying to yourself.

Wrong! My two children check the toilet paper situation before they sit down. If the roll is empty, they'll simply use another bathroom.

Yes, I'm the only one in the entire family who knows how to take an empty toilet paper roll off the holder and replace it with a full roll. It's not a difficult task, but it seems impossible for anyone else in the family to master the technique.

A few months ago I got fed up and bought 12 rolls of toilet paper, four for each bathroom. Then I gathered everyone together for a family conference.

"There are extra rolls of toilet paper in each of the bathroom closets," I said. "When you see an empty roll, I want you to replace it with a full roll. I'm taking a little vacation from that duty. Does everyone understand?"

There were nods and vague responses.

A week later the holders in all three bathrooms were empty, but toilet paper rolls were stacked on the edge of the tubs, the bathroom counters, and on the floor.

Three weeks later we were completely out.

"How is it possible to go for days without using any

toilet paper?" I asked my daughters.

"I've been using the neighbor's bathroom," my older said.

"I've been using the Kleenex," my younger said.

So guess who is back changing the toilet paper rolls? That's right—me!

Mother never told me it would be like this!

18

Tresses just lead to distresses

I read recently that the thing American teen-agers are most worried about is the threat of nuclear war.

You could have fooled me. I thought they worried about their hair more than anything else.

I know quite a few teen-agers, and I haven't heard even one of them mention nuclear war in the past three months. Come to think of it, how many families do you know that discuss things like the SALT talks at the dinner table? Our table conversations are pretty much limited to minor skirmishes over whether someone put too much salt on the mashed potatoes.

Hair is the paramount concern of every teen-ager I know.

Your typical adolescent worries about the cleanliness of hair, the length of hair, the color of hair, the shape of hair, and the condition of hair.

Teen-agers spend 2 hours out of every 24 washing their hair. They spend 10 hours combing it, brushing it, fixing it, spraying it, and primping it. The remaining 12 hours are spent in front of a mirror, watching the hair to make sure none of it gets out of place.

In a drug store, the teen-ager gravitates to the aisle with shampoos, conditioners, sprays, dyes and other concoctions for the hair. After all, when you go through a case of shampoo every month, you've got to keep an eye out for bargains.

Watching television, the teen-ager snaps to attention when an advertisement for a hair product appears on the screen. Every young person knows how important it is to stay abreast of the latest in hair fashion.

During school, the teen-ager visits the bathroom between every class to double check the shape of the hair and to make sure none of that dastardly dandruff is showing on the shoulders.

Teen-agers occasionally engage in conversations with adults, but you can tell that their minds are always on something else—hair.

How do I know? Just try to recall the last time you saw a young boy who wasn't fingering an overly large comb sticking out of the back pocket of his jeans. Or a girl who wasn't brushing her hair at the dining room table, the bus stop, the check-out counter, the library, or the entrance to the mall?

I certainly don't mean to make light of the nuclear war threat. Teen-agers probably do spend a lot of time worrying about such important issues.

I'm sure they are concerned about age (the age they need to be to drive a car). And the economy (whether they're going to be able to stretch their allowance through the end of the week). And housing (how long they have to endure living in their parents' home).

But in reality, those topics are small potatoes when compared with the hair issue. Because with hair, there's so much to worry about!

The locks are either too long or too short. And either condition can result in social ostracism.

If an adolescent was born with gorgeous blond tresses, she will naturally want to dye her hair black and style it with little ringlets. And of course all brunettes worry about blonds having more fun.

To look acceptable, every hair has to be in place. But no teen-ager wants anyone else to know that he or she emptied a full can of hair spray in the bathroom that morning before school.

A teen's hair must have bounce, flair, ummph. Even if it means spending an hour in the shower three times a day. After all, no one is going to see the pruny feet. All eyes will be riveted on the hair!

Of course teen-agers aren't the only ones worried about hair. I know quite a few parents of adolescents who are concerned about all the gray hair they're discovering in the bathroom mirror.

And if you think the gray hair comes from worrying about the threat of nuclear war, you obviously don't have any teen-agers around your house.

19
Dilemma du jour

Every day at about 4 p.m., millions of American women converge upon their local supermarket and wander up and down the aisles aimlessly, searching for something new and different to serve for dinner.

Bored with hamburger and unable to afford steak, they hope against hope that God will invent a new meat. Repulsed at the thought of spending hours baking an apple pie, they pick through frozen cookies and instant pudding. Guilty about the lack of nutrition in their children's diet, they debate whether to buy frozen beans or canned peas.

Put it all together and what have they got? Another uninspiring meal and some more dirty dishes.

So how do you put some excitement into dinner time? Well, you can buy all of Julia Child's cookbooks and spend five hours a day cooking and another three hours a day shopping for food. Or you can get a full-time job and hire a cook to come into your home and prepare the meal for you.

But that's just fantasy. Let's get back to reality.

There I was last week, standing in front of the meat counter at my supermarket, trying to decide between pork chops or ground beef. Every day the decision gets harder to make, and every day I delay it a little longer.

So I'd been standing in the same spot for about five minutes, staring down at the little packages of meat and weighing pork chops and hamburger in my mind. Suddenly my friend Nelda rushed by with a shopping cart full of groceries.

She reached in front of me and grabbed some chicken legs out of the meat counter without a moment's hesitation.

"Nelda," I yelled in astonishment. "How can you make a dinner decision so quickly?"

She motioned me over to the produce department, opened her purse and pulled out a little booklet. The cover said "365 ways to cook chicken and make your dinner more exciting."

Personally, chicken for dinner every day of the year does not exactly make my taste buds tingle with excitement. But just out of curiosity, I thumbed through the book, thinking I might come across something that sounded better than pork chops or hamburger. Actually, it was just another delay tactic.

What really caught my eye, however, was a glossary of terms explaining everything you ever wanted to know about chickens, and quite a bit that you didn't want to know, too.

It suddenly occurred to me that those millions of American women who are searching for a new and different dinner menu really need some help. And I'm the one who's going to give it to them.

So here it is . . . Debby's Dinner Directory. Cut out this information and carry it with you every time you go near the supermarket. It will save you hours of agony.

Debby's Dinner Directory

Steak: This red meat is too expensive, contains too much cholesterol, and may cause cancer, but it is the most wonderful thing God ever created.

Hamburger: The steak of the masses, ground beef never really makes it as a cheap substitute in beef stroganoff, no matter what the cook books may tell you.

Hamburger Helper: A concoction designed to disguise the taste and appearance of ground beef so your family won't realize you are once again serving them hamburger.

Liver: A bloody and disgusting looking red meat that can be prepared in a variety of ways but is invariably described with one word—"Yuckky!"

Chicken: The most versatile food, chicken can be prepared in at least four million different ways and is prized throughout the world for its beautiful breasts.

Fish: A delightful dinner alternative until your child finds the first bone and then picks through the rest of the fish with tweezers and a magnifying glass.

Lobster tail: Something to be eaten only by adults. Children should be encouraged to think lobster may be hazardous to their health.

Vegetables: A wide variety of garden edibles, usually green, that are highly nutritious, extremely delicious, and to which almost all children claim to be highly allergic.

Soup: A great idea when you simply can't decide what to feed the family for dinner. All you need is a can opener.

Sandwiches: When all else fails, peanut butter and jelly is acceptable to just about everyone.

Spaghetti: This delicious food takes eight hours to prepare, one hour to digest, and five months to get off your hips.

Potatoes: An alternative to Stove Top Stuffing, potatoes can be mashed, baked, fried, cooked or boiled. They also come in a box.

Chocolate: The staff of life!

20
The galloping gourmand

Sending a man into a supermarket is like sending a child into a candy store with a pocketful of money.

A woman will go into the supermarket with a two-page list, come out 10 minutes later with two bags of groceries, and tell her husband, "Can you believe I had to pay $48.56 for this?"

A man will go into the supermarket with a list of three basics, come out 75 minutes later with a cart full of goodies, and tell his wife, "You wouldn't believe all the great things they have in that store!"

I don't know what it is, but something about supermarkets turns your average penny-pinching male into an impulse buyer. Most men are so tight they wouldn't even spring for new shoelaces. But steer them down the aisle of a supermarket and their eyes light up like Rudolph's nose.

Over the years I've learned to keep my husband at a distance of at least three blocks from any supermarket. It was, I might add, an expensive lesson.

But one day last month I was making some cookies and I ran out of butter. Since I was covered with flour, there was no alternative.

"Honey, will you go to the store and buy one pound of butter?" I asked. That was at 3:15.

At five o'clock I heard someone tapping on the garage door. I opened the door to see my husband, surrounded by grocery bags, leaning against the wall.

"It's a good thing you answered the door," he said. "I didn't have a free hand to open it."

As he lugged the bags into the kitchen, he said "Wait 'til you see all the goodies I brought home."

"I can't wait," I said with all the enthusiasm I could muster.

The kitchen counter quickly filled up, and goodies began overflowing onto the floor, the table, the stove, and any other empty surface.

"Here's your butter. I also bought some of this unsalted butter, in case you needed a different kind.

"And I thought you might be out of chocolate chips, so I brought home a few extra bags. And look at this neat cookie jar I found at the store.

"Here's some of that delicious imported ice cream. I thought you might like to have some to go with those cookies.

"Oh, I found a box of that delicious chocolate candy that we used to get up north. It's a little expensive, but we deserve a treat now and then."

This is a little hard to take from a man who circled the calendar in black and went into mourning every time they raised the price of first class postage.

"Look what I discovered. You can buy hydroponically grown lettuce in the store. Isn't that something? I brought a few heads home to try.

"And I've always wanted to taste this lingonberry jam. I know the kids like grape jelly, but this was only $1.50 more. And it's made in Scotland, see!"

How can a man who can't pass by a phone booth without checking for leftover change get excited about spending $2.98 for a little jar of lingonberry jam?

"When was the last time you smelled freshly ground coffee? Well I just couldn't pass up the chance to use that machine. I haven't ground coffee since I was a kid. Here's two bags.

"And just look at these beautiful artichokes. They'll be

69

good for dinner. I got this gigantic steak to go with them. Won't this taste good?"

It's hard to believe these words could come out of the same mouth that suggested we live without air conditioning last August to save a few dollars on electricity.

"Here's a real treat. Escargot shells and a little can of snails.

"And wait 'til you taste these fresh strawberries! I got some real whipped cream to go with them.

"How about this . . . three pounds of that special cheese they ship over here from Denmark."

Why couldn't he be in such a good mood on April 15? Maybe he's found some way to write this off on his taxes.

"See these? I bought copies of three different gourmet cooking magazines. They should give you some good ideas.

"I noticed that one of the lights in the chandelier was burnt out so I got six new bulbs.

"And here are new lunch boxes for the kids. Aren't they cute? This one's got Pac-Man on the front, and look at this fancy thermos bottle in the other lunch box."

The dish towels are so old you can see through them, and he went out and bought new lunch boxes for the kids. Isn't that just the way!

"Lucky thing I had my check book with me," he said after all the goodies were stashed away. "Prices sure have skyrocketed since the last time I went shopping."

"I wouldn't worry about it too much," I said as I searched through the refrigerator for the butter. He doesn't know it yet, but he's been permanently retired from the supermarket route. Frankly, I'd rather send my kids to the candy store with a fistful of money.

21
Drowning in peanut butter

How can you tell if a woman has children?

If she's wearing a necklace made of painted macaroni noodles, chances are she's got a kid who just got home from Scout camp.

If she spends half an hour in front of the cereal section of the grocery store going back and forth checking which prizes are in the cereal boxes, you can guess that there is a child at home sitting in front of the television set.

If her grocery cart is stacked high with toilet paper and bleach bottles, it's safe to assume she lives with a pack of kids.

I never realized how obvious motherhood was until some woman looked over at me in the supermarket and asked me how old my children were.

"How do you know I have kids?" I asked her.

"Why else would you be buying four king-size jars of peanut butter?"

"Maybe my husband likes peanut butter," I said.

"Nobody likes that much peanut butter," she replied with a knowing smile. "Besides, I saw you talking with the cookie lady at the bakery section. Only women with kids know the cookie lady by her first name. That's a dead giveaway."

I guess a mother's life is an open book. The butcher knows when you've hit hard times. The mailman knows who your creditors are. And it's downright frightening to think what your child's teacher knows about you.

So now that we have that depressing news out of the way, let's get on with Debby's guide for recognizing women with kids.

If a woman asks you where the potty is when she's looking for the restroom, you can be sure she's got a few toddlers waiting for her at home.

If buying a new toothbrush is the most exciting event of her week, she's been paying attention to the kids too long.

When she's at a cocktail party and she starts talking about the characters on Sesame Street, you can bet she hasn't seen another adult for months.

When the hem of her skirt is held together by Scotch tape, you can tell she's a whiz at patching kids' clothing.

When she knows everyone in the hospital emergency room on a first-name basis, it's obvious that her kids do, too.

How else can you tell if a woman has children at home?

● If the ashtray in her car is crammed full of gum wrappers.

● If she waits for the drive-in bank teller to give her a lollypop.

● If she sticks her right hand out when she makes a quick stop while driving the car.

● If she talks with her hands and says "read my lips."

● If she can reach into an aquarium that looks like a bowl of pea soup and pull out a dead guppy without being squeamish.

● If she buys shoelaces by the gross.

● If she rubs her toes and tells you she's got sore "piggies."

● If the sand on her beach towel is an inch deep and she doesn't seem to mind in the least.

● If she folds her kitchen towels like diapers.

● If she trims the crust off the bread and cuts the sandwich into four little pieces, even if it's for an adult.

● If she thinks of a needle as something to pick out

72

splinters with rather than a sewing tool.

- If the back seat of her car looks like the inside of a garbage truck.
- If you can read the words **WASH ME** through the fingerprints on the sliding glass doors.
- If she locks the door after going inside the bathroom.
- If she flatly refuses to play Monopoly.
- If she crosses to the other side of the mall when she passes the pet store.
- If she goes on a camping trip with a pink sleeping bag covered with little blue Smurfs.
- If her jewelry box contains only baby teeth, painted sea shells and a silver rattle.

22
Cooking the bacon versus bringing it home

I've discovered there's a direct correlation between Reaganomics and the number of housewives out looking for a job.

It may simply be the desire to have those smart little Adolfo suits the First Lady has a fondness for. But I have a suspicion it has something to do with the fact that the dollar just doesn't go as far these days. I know my dollar only goes as far as the supermarket.

For whatever the reason, lots of women who have spent the last decade folding clothes while they watched the soaps are suddenly having to cope with the pressures of a 9-to-5 job in addition to the full-time job at home.

It's not easy. I can tell you from experience, and I'm only working part time. But when the "woman" in the house isn't home all day to take care of the household chores, it takes a while for everyone to make the adjustment.

Any working woman soon finds that she has to re-evaluate priorities, and that includes dinner. I used to spend hours each day worrying about what to serve for dinner. Now that I'm working, I've got that time span down to a mere five minutes. Unless, of course, there is an extra long line at the McDonald's drive-in window.

Families with working mothers quickly learn to live on

junk food and boxes of goodies from take-out restaurants. Wise mothers are always careful to keep some parsley in the refrigerator so they can garnish the paper plates before putting them on the table.

And I've found out that if you turn the television on while you eat dinner, it will be months before your family notices they're eating the same food night after night.

My husband discovered the bitter truth while taking out the garbage.

"Do you realize that before you started working, we averaged four big cans of garbage a week," he said one night. "And now we're down to a little Baggie full of dog scraps and a garbage can full of greasy fried chicken boxes. Isn't that odd?"

"It certainly is, dear," I said. "I guess when I'm out of the house all day, I just don't generate as much trash."

Time becomes more valuable for working mothers.

When an ice cube drops on the kitchen floor, you learn to kick it under the refrigerator rather than take the time to bend over and pick up the pieces. After all, who's going to be looking under the refrigerator for little puddles of water anyway?

Clean clothes also become more valuable. In our house the kids have resorted to flipping a coin each morning to decide who gets the clean underwear.

The alarming increase in dirty clothes was so bad I had to go out and buy two more laundry baskets just to handle the overflow. When they fill up, I don't know what I'm going to do.

On a few occasions I have gotten around to using the washing machine. But ironing is absolutely out of the question.

If I find something in the stack of clean clothes that needs to be ironed, I just stick it back in the dirty clothes and hope no one will notice. But that's a trick I've been getting away with for years. In fact my husband has shirts that have never seen the light of day. I can't imagine why

they bother to make anything but permanent press fabric, can you?

And at some point a working mother will realize that cleanliness isn't necessarily all that important. I discovered that the weekly housecleaning chores I used to put off until the end of the month can actually be put off indefinitely.

We've adopted a new motto in our house: YOU TOUCH IT, YOU DUST IT! It's amazing how well it works.

In the final analysis, however, who truly cares if there is week-old wild rice buried in the dining room carpet? The dog will take care of the problem.

Naturally, working mothers can't escape the guilt of

somehow failing to accomplish everything that needs to be accomplished during the day. Just last week I was lamenting with my daughter about the condition of our house.

"Don't worry, Mother," she said with concern. "Things really aren't much different than before you started working."

Why does the truth always hurt so much?

23
All things to all people

Let's hear it for Supermom.

You all know her. She's the perfect mother.

She cooks. Her family enjoys delicious meals every day, from French toast and freshly squeezed orange juice in the morning to beef stroganoff and spinach souffle in the evening. If the kids want fried chicken, she prepares it at home instead of paying a quick visit to the Colonel. And the menu is always varied, with something to appeal to every family member.

She cleans. Her kitchen is spotless, and her pots and pans shine. There are never any dog bones under the sofa or dead bugs in the corner. The kids never have a chance to write nasty messages with cherry popsicles on the bathroom mirrors because she wipes them off each day with a solution of vinegar and water. The front of her refrigerator is spotless.

She's organized. She knows which pills the dog gets at 9 a.m. and which pills the kid gets at 4 p.m., and she never gets them mixed up. Her spice cabinet is arranged in alphabetical order, and her shoes are in clear plastic boxes in the top of the closet.

She's patient. When the kids bring in a bucket of sand and turn the coffee table into a sandbox, she just laughs. When her husband spends Thursday night in a fishing boat instead of at the school concert, she understands. When it's bedtime and her daughter announces she forgot about

the bunny costume she needs for tomorrow's school play, she grabs a needle and thread and spends hours sewing cotton onto a white sheet so her daughter will have the best bunny costume in the class.

She's clever. At Christmas time she makes candles out of broken crayons and leftover ketchup bottles. At Easter she turns pipe cleaners into bunnies. Her beautifully decorated Easter eggs are always the talk of the neighborhood egg hunt. The rest of the year she makes her own soap, sews her own slipcovers, and turns her garden into a topiary work of art.

Her children are obedient. They never beg for candy at the checkout line in the supermarket. They never lose their underwear at summer camp and they never scream "look at that fat lady" in a crowded department store. They make good grades and they perform on command.

She's involved. In addition to being president of the PTA, secretary of the garden club, and chairwoman of the church carnival committee, she has time to help with several fund-raising campaigns, participate in a walk-a-thon, wash cars to raise money for the new theater building, and bake 12 dozen cookies for the Boy Scout meeting.

Not only that, but Supermom is the family chauffer, janitor, nurse, maid and teacher. She's never too fat, and always well-dressed for any occasion. She's a considerate neighbor, a thoughtful daughter, and a terrific lover, too!

How do I know so much about Supermom? Well, I've read about her in magazines and books, seen her on television and in the movies, and watched her on thousands of commercials. So I know she exists.

But frankly, I've always had trouble identifying with her.

One look at my oven and I know I'll never win the Good Housekeeping seal of approval. In fact that's why I stopped cooking seven months ago. The grease had built up so much that I was risking my life every time I turned the oven on. So now I know every fast-food clerk in town on a first-name basis.

My husband learned long ago that if he wanted white shirts without wrinkles, he had better send them to the laundry. I lost track of the iron in 1979.

1979 was also the year I lost track of my patience. Everything the kids do disturbs me. I just can't understand why they can't get along. It's like living in a war zone.

No, I've sadly come to the realization that I'll never be a Supermom. The "happily-ever-after" existence is out of the question.

On a scale of 1 to 10, with Beaver Cleaver's mom as a

80

10, and Joan Crawford as a 1, I'd give myself about a 3.

But I'm not too worried. Looking around, I see that I'm in good company.

24
Heart-a-tax

Nothing is more taxing on a marriage than April 15.

That magic date pits husband against wife in a battle that exposes all the little peccadillos of living together.

Uncle Sam probably has no idea how many marriages have hit the rocks due to his annual accounting requirement. Preparing the 1040 forms is no doubt the biggest hurdle for three-fourths of the couples in America today.

Wives probably get the worst end of it. At least I know one wife who does—me! When my husband finally gets around to tackling the income tax each year, there's just no living with him!

The hardest task is finding the motivation to start. That motivation usually comes magically during the first week in April, when the government starts giving those stern warnings about the upcoming deadline for filing.

The second-hardest chore is finding all the receipts, records, accounts, canceled checks and bank statements from the previous year. That's when tempers really start to flare.

You see, when it comes to organization, it's a toss-up which of us is the worst.

My husband claims his procedure is the best. He throws receipts and other tax records into a big box throughout the year. The box may move from time to time. In January, it's beside his desk. In March, it's next to the bed. By July, it's stuck in some closet. When December rolls around, the box is usually out in the garage, buried under the fishing rods, painting drop cloths and old National Geographics.

As disjointed as his procedure is to me, my disorganization seems infinitely more frustrating to him.

I know where all the receipts and records are . . . it just takes me a little time to dig them out.

For instance, the dentist's bill for all that work on my receding gums last July is in the bathroom drawer, right beside the dental floss that was purchased with good intentions but never used. And the receipt for September's day care service is stuck in the box with all of those summer clothes that don't fit my younger daughter any more.

Gasoline receipts are stored in about six purses located in various closets throughout the house, and the canceled checks are in the drawer in my dresser . . . no, make that on the kitchen counter . . . wait, I think they're in the top drawer of the desk . . . no, maybe it's the end table in the living room. Well, we'll find them eventually.

Record-keeping has never really been my forte. I've never been known for writing notes in my checkbook on the amount of the check and to whom it was made out. I always tell myself I'll do it later when I'm not so rushed. I've always been good at lying to myself.

Once my husband finally gets everything rounded up and he is drowning in a sea of canceled checks, receipts and records, things really get sticky.

"Would you kindly explain to me why you've entered $385 for a new pair of sunglasses when the doctor only charged you $65?" he asked me one day.

Without total recall, it's hard to piece it all together, but I tried.

"Well, Beth forgot her lunchbox that day, so I had to rush it over to school on my way to the eye doctor," I told him. "I forgot about the 15-mile-per-hour speed limit in the school zone, so I had to pay $25 for the speeding ticket."

"That brings it down to $295. Where did the other expenses come from?"

"When I finally got through with my eye exam, I went out and found that somebody had backed into the side of my car. It cost $220 to get it fixed. Don't you remember?"

"That takes care of $310. How about the rest?"

"I was so upset I had to go to the drug store to buy some aspirin."

"Aspirin only costs $1.95," he said. "Where did the rest of the $75 go?"

"Well, while I was in the drug store, I saw a darling pair of sandals. They cost $15. And the picture frame cost $9.95. And the candy came to $3.50. And the . . ."

"Hold it," he said. "How did candy enter the picture?"

"Well, I had to give Andrea something to keep her quiet. Her screaming was driving everyone mad."

"Just why was she screaming?"

"Because she accidentally broke the new sunglasses I bought her. She wanted new sunglasses to match my new sunglasses. They were only $7.98."

"OK," he said in exasperation. "That makes $385 for new sunglasses. Now how about explaining this $239 charge for emergency treatment for your house plants."

The inquisition goes on and on.

One thing I've learned, though: taxes depress even the most well-adjusted male. So there's just no use in trying to lighten the load with little jokes.

"We've just got to figure out some way to pay less taxes next year," my husband shouted as he threw the calculator into the pool.

"Lucky for you I stopped at the book store this afternoon and picked up this handy guide to tax shelters," I told him.

"All we need to do is choose one of the top ten on the list. There's an aardvark farm in Anaheim, or a Chrysler dealership in Kalamazoo, or a professional shuffleboard team in Sheboygan, or an ice rink for senior citizen hockey players in Buffalo, or a . . ."

He didn't find it a bit amusing.

25
Slam, bam, thank you ma'am

I used to be a nervous wreck.

Screaming kids, a dirty house, even a mere spill in the kitchen was enough to make my temper as tense as a tight-rope.

But all that changed last Christmas when Santa Claus brought me his own version of Valium—Intellivision's Space Battle.

I've not shouted or screamed at my family since.

Dirty dishes may be piled up in the sink, kids may be drawing with finger paints on my wall, and the visiting baby may be pulling my dog's hair out, but I don't even notice. I'm too busy taking out all my aggressions on the aliens from another planet that are whizzing across my television screen.

In my mind each enemy battleship becomes a dirty kitchen floor or another visitor with the flu, and I fire on them with the vengeance of a woman scorned. Ah, it feels so good!

BAM! There goes the Christmas guest that burned a hole in my sofa. **ZAP!** There goes the house-guest who spilled grape juice on the living room rug. **POW!** There goes the store that charged me $73 for a toy that broke one hour after Santa Claus arrived.

George Plimpton was right. These television games have got to be good for you.

Granted, I'm going blind after countless hours of staring at the TV screen and I'm getting curvature of the spine from hunching over the controls. The manual "fire" button will be forever indented in my badly blistered finger. Psychologically, however, it works wonders.

And just think of all the great things you can learn with these electronic video games. Why I've become so adept at shooting down objects from outer space that I bet I'll be invaluable to the Defense Department the moment we are invaded by aliens.

I've learned to read the radar screen so well I could take command of a control tower if we ever have to suffer through another air traffic controllers strike.

Yes, when George Plimpton, in his best Harvard accent, describes my game as the thinking man's game of total destruction in those television commercials, I stand up and give the old "Paper Lion" an electronic salute.

The fact that our family room now sounds like a penny arcade doesn't bother me. But my husband is a bit concerned.

Just the other day he came home from work to find me glued to the television set, destroying another squadron of alien fighters.

"What's for dinner," he asked.

"I don't know." **ZAP!** "I haven't had a chance . . ." **BAM!** ". . . to get to the store." **ZAP! ZAP!**

"Well I'm starved," he said.

"Go out and get some fried chicken." **ZAP!** "I've got two more alien squadrons that are closing in on the mother ship." **BAM!** "And would you mind picking up the kids from school." **ZAP! ZAP!** "I forgot to get them this afternoon." **BAM!**

He got back just as I was starting another Space Battle game.

"You go ahead and eat, honey." **BAM! BAM!** "I just dispatched a fighter squadron and it's ready to go to battle."

After the kids were in bed, my husband walked over and stood in front of the TV screen.

"What are you doing," I screamed. "That alien laser just nailed my missile." **BOOM!**

"This has got to stop," he said, shutting off the television. "You haven't been out of the house for days. All you do is sit and shoot at those silly spaceships all day. What about real life?"

"This is real life," I snipped, feeling sudden frustration at being deprived of my battle screen. "I'm preparing for the future. You're living in the past."

We could both sense an electronic stalemate. As he walked away I quickly reached for my hand control unit, pressed the reset button, and was into another space battle.

Two alien squadrons were approaching the danger zone boundary and the screen turned red as he went off to bed.

"I'll be in in a few minutes," I yelled as I hit the reset button and dispatched another fighter. **ZAP! ZAP!** "Just as soon as I destroy all these aliens."

26
Dust to dust

There are only two things that can motivate me to give my house a thorough cleaning. One is a **"FOR SALE"** sign in my front yard. The other is a party.

The **"FOR SALE"** sign gets better results. Once I realize that hundreds of people will be inspecting my house with a magnifying glass, I launch a "search and destroy" mission, hunting for dirt that hasn't been seen for years.

But let's face it, how many times a year can you list your house with a realtor? It gets to be a real drag. So periodically I throw small parties, not so much to entertain friends, mind you, but more out of necessity.

A party provides the incentive I need to dig out the vacuum cleaner and scrape the moldy fingerprints off the sliding glass doors.

You see, I've never been known as Nelly Neat. There are lots of things I'd rather do than clean house . . . like taking a dozen 6-year-olds to the movies, or figuring out the income tax, or spending a rainy week in a tent with my daughter's Girl Scout troop, watching the lake rise.

Not that I'm a messy person. It's just that I happen to live in a messy house. And no matter how hard I try, the place just won't stay the way a house is supposed to look.

I could spend an entire week cleaning, and as soon as I throw in the sponge, I'm once again tripping over someone's tennis shoes and trying to figure out how the ketchup hit the television screen.

You wouldn't believe the treasures that lie beneath the couch cushions. And I suspect that new and secret forms of life now exist in my refrigerator. I know they're already living in my oven.

While house cleaning has never really been my bag, I've discovered over the years that there are three levels of cleaning you have to deal with. I have no trouble with the first level, but the second and third require professional help.

Level one is what I call clutter. Clutter is unmade beds, that disgusting hairbrush on the kitchen counter, the detergent that is spilled across the top of the clothes drier, dirty laundry spilling over the top of one basket and clean laundry spilling over the top of another basket, a stack of magazines waiting to be read, and a variety of shoes in every room. The shoes, of course, never match.

Clutter is easy to cope with, especially if you have a lot of closets in your house. You should see my closets!

Level two is what I call messiness. Messiness is broken cookies in the air conditioning vent, fingerprints in a 12-inch circle around the light switches, grease on the oven window that's so thick you can't see in, and a tic-tac-toe game that someone played on the glass shower door last summer.

I never realized what messiness was until I had kids. Before the kids were born, I wasn't afraid to look under the sofa. Now I'm never sure what's lurking under there.

Level three is real dirt. That's the stuff you find if you look in the tracks of your sliding glass doors, or the corners of your shower, or behind your bed's headboard, or—worst of all—underneath your refrigerator.

These areas are only tackled by cleaning fanatics, who carry toothpicks into the shower so they can clean out the mineral deposits in the shower head.

I'm sure you know some cleaning fanatics. They use Q-

tips to scrape the dirt out from around the buttons on the blender. They wash out the light-diffusion bowls every time a dead fly lands inside. They never tolerate bread crumbs in the bottom of the toaster.

Fanatics work on a schedule, cleaning a different room each day of the week so that dirt never has a chance to settle. That sounds good in theory, but if I cleaned the kitchen only on Monday, I'm afraid I wouldn't be able to make it to the kitchen sink by Sunday. The dustballs would be so big by Thursday that the kids would be rolling them down the kitchen floor and yelling "STRIKE!"

The only answer is to send out invitations to a party and get ready for a concentrated house-cleaning. Of course if I really want motivation, I could always invite my mother to the party. She's meticulous. But isn't every mother?

27
How to eat like a child

It takes a special kind of appetite to eat dinner at the same table with children. That, and a strong stomach.

Kids seem to have a different attitude toward food. They look at eating as a necessary evil, kind of like brushing teeth. And they're not about to make dinner time any easier than bedtime.

For instance, take vegetables . . . **PLEASE!**

Most adults look at vegetables as a tasty addition to dinner, a source of vitamins, a real treat. Most kids, however, look at vegetables as the ultimate challenge.

I know for a fact that my little girl spends the first nine hours of every day wondering how she can avoid eating the vegetables on her dinner plate. That's her only concern from 8 a.m. until 5 p.m.

As soon as she sees the vegetables, she goes into her righteous indignation routine. "Do I have to eat those? I don't like them. Why do we have to have those yukky vegetables? Can't I have peanut butter instead?"

Five little green peas doesn't seem like too much for a 6-year-old kid to handle, does it? Well, in her eyes I might as well have put five bushels on her plate.

"Oh, Mom!" she says with her arms up in the air as if I have just dealt her the greatest injustice in the world.

As the rest of the family enjoys the meal, she proceeds to split each pea into three pieces. Then she removes the skin and carefully puts it in a little pile on the side of her plate.

She lifts a piece of pea no bigger than a speck of pepper onto her fork and puts it in her mouth, where it stays for a good five minutes.

At her sister's urging she gulps some milk to make the pea go down a little easier. But after swallowing half a glass of milk, the little green dot is still on the end of her tongue.

An hour later she finally holds her nose, stuffs the remaining peas in her mouth, takes a big swig of milk and somehow manages to make everything disappear.

Carrots aren't much better. She can chew a mouthful of raw carrots for what seems to be forever, but one sneeze sends little orange shreds in every direction.

And how does she eat corn? Kernel by kernel by kernel by kernel by kernel. . . .

Mashed potatoes are another struggle. First she scoops out a little hole in the middle and waits for it to fill up with melted butter. Then she eats the butter with a spoon. When the butter is all gone, she can't eat the potatoes because "there's no butter on them."

When that ploy doesn't work, she starts playing with the potatoes. By the time everyone else at the table is finished with dinner, her plate looks like a relief map of the Antarctic (minus the butter, of course).

She uses the divide and conquer technique with green beans. First she divides them up into little piles. Then she moves them around on her plate the way some people play checkers. After 30 minutes of such activity, she asks if she has eaten enough to get dessert. In fact, she has not eaten a single bite.

The strange eating habits are not limited to vegetables. I've seen her make a dish of spaghetti look like a bowl of vegetable soup. She waves a fork around like Leonard Bernstein conducting the New York Philharmonic Orchestra. She even dumps soy sauce on her applesauce.

Her best trick, however, is with chicken. How many letters can you make out of chicken bones? My daughter has mastered nearly the entire alphabet, and with just the wings. Try to top that for good dinner conversation.

And of course there's the dish of ice cream. Any child in his right mind would never dream of eating ice cream while it's still cold and hard. No, ice cream has to melt before it's any good.

My daughter has the unnerving habit of chopping up ice cream into little pieces so that it melts faster. That way it can drip down her chin, bounce off her little hand and land on the carpet, the chair, the table and sometimes on her bib.

My friend Nelda says I'm lucky. Her teen-agers are eating her out of house and home. "Just you wait," she told me the other day when I was complaining about meal time. "In a few years you'll be wishing they were 6 years old again."

Frankly, I'll believe it when I see it!

28

Raindrops keep falling in the trunk

When it rains, it pours inside the trunk of my husband's car.

Yes, it's true. Because of a mysterious leak somewhere, each time the heavens open up, the trunk fills up—with water.

I was the first to notice it. One day I happened to be following him on the highway and I noticed that the tail lights on his car looked like fish bowls. Each time he turned a corner, a little wave would go from side to side in the tail light. As a matter of fact, it looked just like those little wave machines you used to buy in the novelty stores.

When I pointed out this little oddity, he opened the lid of the trunk and found a thin layer of dirty, rusty water covering the floor.

After draining the tail lights and sponging up the water in the trunk, he promptly forgot about it. Until the next rain storm, that is.

"I could hear the water rushing from one side to the other every time I went around a bend," he said that afternoon as he was scooping about an inch of water from the trunk. "There must be a leak somewhere."

Now finding a leak in my husband's car is like trying to figure out who shot J. R.—there are so many possibilities. To give you some idea of the enormity of the problem, let me briefly describe the car. During better times (about 10 years ago) it was green. Now half of the body is rust and what little green metal there is left is on the verge of joining the rust side of the battle.

Whenever my husband gets in his car, shuts the door and drives away, there is always a little pile of rust that is left behind in the driveway. Each day the pile that falls from the car gets bigger. One day, I suspect, he will get in the car, slam the door, and the whole car will crumble around him.

So you can see that finding the one hole that lets rain water inside the trunk is no small challenge. He puttied here and plastered there and even tried to tape some holes shut around the trunk area. But nothing helped. In fact things got worse.

With each rain storm—and you know how many rain storms there are in the summer months in Florida—the amount of water he had to bail out of the trunk of his car got worse. By August he was dumping gallons of water on the driveway each evening.

As the water level reached three inches, one of our daughters suggested he keep goldfish in the trunk and advertise the car as an aquarium on wheels. When the water hit the five-inch mark, our other daughter asked her dad if she could sail her toy boat in his trunk. At seven inches I suggested he drill a hole in the trunk so the water could drain out, but he was afraid of drilling through the gas tank by mistake.

One day after a particularly bad rain shower he was heading home from work and had to suddenly slam on the brakes. The momentum somehow sent some of the water splashing out of the trunk and onto the floor in the back seat area, creating two little puddles.

The next morning he went out the front door as usual, suddenly returned to drag me outside, and pointed at the car. There was more condensation on the inside of the windows than on the outside. And it was the kind of condensation that you just can't wipe off. It kept dripping.

"As the day progressed," he told us at the dinner table that night, "the heat turned the inside of the car into a steam bath."

For days he was airing out the car during the day and dumping water from the trunk at night. And his mood showed it, I might add.

About two weeks later the same thing happened again, only this time the water that ended up on the floor of the car served as a breeding ground for the mosquitoes. They were everywhere!

After a weekend of rain, I knew to expect the worst.

"We've either got to solve this problem or get rid of this car," he shouted, along with some other choice words that I won't repeat here. I could see the spare tire floating around in about 10 inches of water. The jack was coated with rust and water was dripping from the tail lights.

"Have patience," I urged him. After all, the dry season is just around the corner!

29
Off-the-wall decorating tips

Have you ever had the urge to throw out everything in your house and start fresh?

Just once, instead of trying to find a new sofa that will match the dirty gold carpet and the faded, flowered chair, I'd like to be able to buy a pretty new sofa and then get everything else to go with it.

I don't mean just the basics . . . I mean everything, from the ashtrays to the art on the walls. What fun it would be!

Of course it's only a dream. My decorating experience has been limited to finding just the right shaped pillow to cover up the grape juice stain on the arm rest of the sofa, and matching up packing crates for book cases.

My one big challenge was the bathroom. I spent months trying to find towels that matched the mildew on the shower curtain. Finally I gave up and cut the bottom off the shower curtain.

What I've learned through the years is that you never really get your house just the way you want it. It's sort of a trial-and-error process. And when you err, like buying the wrong sofa, it's a lifetime sentence.

When we moved into our house six years ago, the walls of the family room were covered with ugly brown grass cloth.

"Let's tear that off and put up some pretty wallpaper," I told my husband.

But he refused to rip the grass cloth off the walls.

"How could you even think of destroying such expensive wallcovering," he asked me.

It took months to find brown carpeting that would match the grass cloth. And even more months to find a sofa that would blend with the carpeting and wallcovering. And I never did like the combination.

Just a few weeks after we bought the sofa, the grass cloth started peeling off the walls. Either the humidity was too much to take, or the grass cloth was hurt by my insults.

Our feeble attempt at gluing it back on the walls made the grass cloth look even worse.

So we were forced to find a new wallcovering that would match the bland brown carpet and the not-so-beautiful sofa. Not a pleasant task, I might add.

If you've ever shopped for wallpaper, you know that it's an impossible job. You have your choice of 3,500 books of samples to look through, and you can never tell a book by its cover.

"Can I help you look for something," the clerk always says with a smile.

"I'm looking for something with stripes."

"Well, you might want to look through those 900 books on the right-hand shelf," she says as she walks away, always knowing the right time to make an exit.

After spending four months of my life in wallpaper stores searching for a suitable replacement for the grass cloth in the family room, I discovered a paper that would look awfully good in my daughter's bathroom, so I bought it.

This purchase led me to the discovery of the snowball theory of decorating: You can never fix up just one room of your house; it always leads to something else.

As soon as the wallpaper in her bathroom was up, I realized that new towels and a shower curtain were a must.

It didn't take long for my daughter to comment on how

dreary her bedroom looked next to the beautifully decorated bathroom. Of course she needed new bedspreads and drapes, and a new coat of paint on the walls.

I defy you to paint just one room of your house. Then all the other rooms look like the inside of a dirty oven.

So in the next 10 months we ended up painting the hallway, the guest bedroom, my other daughter's bedroom, the living room and the dining room. All the while the grass cloth in the family room was slowly peeling away from the walls.

"We've got to do something with the family room," I told my husband one day as I was ironing the wallcovering, trying to get it to stick to the wall.

So back to the wallpaper store I went to scan through 1,200 new sample books. That's when I came across a paper that would be perfect for the dining room and the front hallway.

"But what about the family room?" my husband asked as I was showing him the 12 rolls of wallpaper that would cover the dining room.

So now almost every room in the house has been tampered with. After spending $4,987 on paint, wallpaper, drapes, curtains and assorted decorator items, the house looks a little cleaner but about the same.

But the grass cloth is beginning to hang like the drapes, in folds across the family room walls.

"Why don't you stop at the wallpaper store some day and try to find something for these walls," my husband said the other day.

I may be naive, but I'm not stupid!

30
Motherhood: justice but no peace

Being a mother is a lot like being a judge—only the pay isn't as good.

Every day I've got dozens of cases to hear, and the two little attorneys that are running around our house disguised as children are surprisingly convincing.

No matter how fair and impartial I try to be, one child is always unhappy with my decision.

It starts with breakfast.

"Mommy, Beth got more cereal than I did."

"No I didn't. Your bowl has more in it."

"It does not!"

"Yes it does!"

Any person who has witnessed such a scene will realize why it's not unusual to see a bleary-eyed mother bent over the kitchen table carefully counting Fruit Loops so that each bowl contains exactly the same number.

And it ends at bedtime.

"How come she gets to stay up later than me?"

"'Cause I'm bigger than you."

"Not that much bigger."

"I am too!"

"Mommy, can I just stay up a little later?"

The arguing between two young children never ends. If one has a bigger piece of cake than the other, a debate

101

starts. And it always ends up in a mother's lap.

The other day as I was serving the kids grapefruit, I told myself it was the perfect solution to the breakfast battle because both grapefruit halves were exactly the same size.

"How come Andrea got more sugar on her grapefruit than I did?" my daughter asked indignantly.

Never one to miss an opportunity, my younger one said "because I'm nicer than you are."

One good retort demands another, so Beth announced that she was sweeter so she didn't need as much sugar.

"You are not!"

"Yes I am!"

"Mommy, is Beth sweeter than I am?"

Now how can a mother make a choice like that?

Often the decisions I have to make are easy. Take the mail, for instance. For some reason the highlight of Andrea's day is the thrill of taking the mail out of the mailbox and bringing it in the house.

Once Beth realized how important the job was to Andrea, she decided she wanted to try it, too. For weeks they would argue all the way home from school about who would "get the mail." It was unbearable!

Finally I issued my decision: they would take turns. That solved the problem of "You got the mail for the last four days so it's my turn this week." Except for holidays, which mess up their schedule.

"It's not fair, Mommy. They didn't deliver mail on Thursday and that was my day to get it," Andrea told me in tears Friday as Beth had the day-after-Thanksgiving mail in her hands. Justice just has to be blind!

And for two children who can never seem to remember to make their beds in the morning, they have a remarkable ability to recall past injustices.

They can remember who got to lick the beaters the last time I made a cake (about four months ago); who got the biggest balloon at the fair last Spring; who received more Christmas presents last year; and who ended up with the biggest end of the wishbone for the past five Thanksgivings.

"Mommy," my younger daughter said as she plopped herself in my lap last weekend, "how come you always talk to Beth first?"

"What do you mean," I asked her. "I don't always talk to Beth first."

"Yes you do. And you give her dinner first, and you answer her questions first, and you kiss her first, and you give her vitamins first, and . . ."

What's a mother to do but suffer through it? If this is the way Sandra Day O'Connor made it to the Supreme Court, I give her a lot of credit. As for myself, I'm ready to hang up my robe and retire!

31
Manners for minors

I learned long ago that the easiest children to raise are somebody else's children. Now I'm just trying to survive my own.

In infancy, it's just the small things. So what if the kid likes to play in the toilet. He'll grow out of it. Who cares if he pulls the dog's hair. The dog's going to shed anyway.

Toddlers are cute, no matter how bad they are.

"Oh, how precious. Tommy drew a picture of a bird on our bedroom wall with lipstick."

But the preschool stage is a killer.

Just the other day I had my little girl at the supermarket and we ran into a friend. Now for some reason, it's not enough that I say hello. I want my little girl to say hello, too.

Nothing.

"Say hello to Mrs. Jones."

Nothing.

"Take your finger out of your nose and say hello to Mrs. Jones."

Nothing.

"I said 'say hello to Mrs. Jones.'"

Nothing but a small glare. At least there was eye contact.

By this time I realize I should have ignored my child and carried on a conversation by myself. But suddenly it was a challenge to make my daughter say hello.

So I pleaded.

"Please say hello to Mrs. Jones."

And I threatened.

"If you don't say hello to Mrs. Jones, I'm putting this candy back on the shelf."

And I cajoled.

"Why don't you be Mommy's nice girl and say hello to Mrs. Jones."

By this time, the ice cream in Mrs. Jones' shopping cart is beginning to drip onto the wilted lettuce, and we are both looking for a way to end this ridiculous confrontation.

But my child has now retreated behind my skirt and refuses to face anyone but the cookie lady.

"Tell you what. You say hello to Mrs. Jones and I'll get you a big cookie to take home."

After a long hesitation, I hear something.

"Lo." It was barely audible.

Mrs. Jones, an obvious sadist, said "What? I couldn't hear you."

Now I have two choices. I can say something like "That's her way of saying hello," or I can look at my daughter and say "Speak up so Mrs. Jones can hear you."

Why I chose the latter alternative, I'll never know. I guess something in me just won't take the easy way out.

So we start again.

"Say hello loud enough so Mrs. Jones can hear you."

Nothing.

"Please darling. Mommy's in a hurry. The people behind us are anxious to check out. Mrs. Jones has other things to do in life than wait around for you to say hello. So give her a great big hello and let's go."

I reached down and pinched her leg. She let out with a loud scream. I said, "That's great. Good to see you, Mrs. Jones. I've got to be running. Say hello to your daughter for me." I hurried out of the store.

I guess sometimes you have to take drastic measures to teach manners to minors.

105

32
Don't point the finger if you're all thumbs

When it comes to being handy around the house, I must have been on the telephone when God was passing out skills. I was probably talking to the refrigerator repairman.

My husband isn't much better. His idea of a tool box is the yellow pages. He can repair anything as long as he has the right telephone numbers.

During the past 10 years we have saved thousands of dollars through our carefully planned program of do-it-yourself home improvements—we avoid them!

My husband refuses to fix anything on the theory that he usually doesn't know what he's doing, and there are always people who need the work.

I used to object, but after a few frustrating experiences, I have learned to live with broken stuff around our house.

If there is something seriously wrong, like when the refrigerator starts squirting water all over the kitchen floor, I quickly call the appropriate repairman. It may be expensive up front, but it's always cheaper in the end.

Life wasn't always that simple.

Our first house was 70 years old, and so were the pipes. They were made of lead, and they tended to bulge.

One weekend the pipe in the basement started to drip. It wasn't a bad drip, but I thought it should be fixed.

My husband looked in his tool box. He had a choice of

a hammer, a pair of pliers, a screwdriver, a wrench, and a cute little saw. He decided on the wrench, which proved to be a serious error in judgment.

One tiny turn of the wrench sent water spraying in every direction. It took me five minutes to dog paddle my way over to the main shut-off valve.

Since it was the first night of a three-day holiday weekend, and the thought of living without water that long gave me a quick case of diarrhea, we ended up calling the plumber.

Naturally, he got triple overtime for making an emergency call on a holiday weekend. But in my book it was worth every penny of the $129.50 just to have the water turned back on.

Undeterred by such a minor setback, several months later my husband brought home an under-the-counter dishwasher, announcing that he planned to install it himself.

His first major project quickly became his last major project. He made it through four paragraphs of instructions before he threw the directions in the garbage and called the appliance store. It took two repairmen three hours to pick their way through the nuts and bolts scattered across the kitchen floor before they had the dishwasher churning out clean dishes.

The tool box disappeared for more than a year. Then one cold winter night, I noticed the heating ducts that ran through the ceiling of our basement were listing away from the little wall vents.

"Why don't you just pound a nail or two around the heating ducts to hold them tight?" I said, standing back as he aimed the hammer.

One quick tap was all it needed. Everything started collapsing. I raised my arms and suddenly the heating system for the entire house was resting on my shoulders. I felt like Charles Atlas.

As each section of heating duct pulled away from the ceiling, the stress would force another section down. Pretty soon I was sitting on the floor of the basement in a cloud of dust and a pile of dirt amid what seemed like miles of foil-coated ductwork.

It took days to get everything straightened out.

About eight years ago I gave my husband a home workshop encyclopedia, a wonderful work of literature that spells out in the simplest terms how to tackle such home repairs as changing a lightbulb and putting a nut on a bolt.

With Volume IV in one hand and a screwdriver in the other, he finally learned how to put a new washer on a faucet, thereby saving $35 each time we had a drip.

Things went fine until we moved to Florida and he finally encountered modern plumbing.

"What is that?" he asked me, staring blankly at a shower stall with no hot or cold handles, only a single chrome wheel.

"That" turned out to be his downfall.

He pressed the wheel and nothing happened.

He turned the wheel and nothing happened.

He pulled on the wheel and a spray of water suddenly filled the room, drenching us both.

"The beauty of these new faucets is that they never need new washers," the plumber told us as he showed us how to turn the water off.

What he didn't tell us, however, is that sometimes those little chrome wheels get stuck. And heaven help you if it's on hot when it gets stuck!

These little chrome wheels may not need washers, but they do need a skilled plumber to repair them. My husband adjusted the faucet in our bathroom last year, and I haven't had a cool shower since.

Turn the little arrow to hot and warm water flows out. Turn the little arrow to cold and the water gets even hotter. If I'm really desperate for a cool bath, I can always jump into the pool.

Despite all the setbacks, my husband isn't intimidated by everyone else's tales of how easy it is to install linoleum or build a book case. He takes it in stride.

"After all," he tells any Mr. Fix-it who will listen, "my refusal to take hammer and screwdriver in hand is a patriotic act that will pump a few bucks directly into the sagging economy."

Isn't modesty wonderful?

33

Look! Up in the sky! It's Super Roach!

As if killer bees weren't enough, now we have to get ready for "Super Roach."

Yes, it's true. Exterminators in Alabama have discovered a new, hardy, resilient breed of cockroach. They didn't waste any time in naming it Super Roach.

It seems this particular strain of cockroach is so tough that most poisons and insecticides don't even slow it down. Only a fast foot or old age can kill Super Roach, they say.

The good news is that Super Roach is still in Birmingham. The bad news is that it's only a matter of time until he eats his way south to Florida.

I know a good story when I hear one, so I flew to Birmingham to interview Super Roach. I tracked him down in a restaurant not far from the airport.

"The exterminators say you're invincible," I told him. "Is it true?"

Super Roach put down the piece of apple pie he was eating.

"Well, I have a slight problem with Kryptonyte, but other than that, very little can even faze me."

I asked him about his favorite foods.

"I eat anything," he said. "Toothpaste, television cables, baseboards, you name it! But my real weakness is Coke.

You know how people always leave a few drops of Coke in those cans they throw away. I've finished off so many bottles I've become addicted to the stuff."

"How did you end up in Birmingham," I asked him.

"Well I heard that Atlanta was the Coke capital of the world, so I set off in that direction. But then on the outskirts of Birmingham I met the cutest little cockroach you ever did see. It was true love, and I've been here for months."

"Where are you going from here," I asked.

"A friend of mine told me about a new kind of Coke they have in Miami. He said it comes in a white powder instead of the usual brown liquid. So I'm planning to head for Florida next week."

Super Roach swung off his cape and showed me his battle plan.

"I'm going to munch my way through Montgomery, tear into Tallahassee, gorge myself in Gainesville, and make oatmeal out of Orlando. From that point on, Florida is mine."

"How many followers do you have?" I asked him.

"Millions!—Millions of roaches who are sick and tired of being portrayed as dummies on those television commercials. Millions of roaches who are fed up with just getting the crumbs in life. Millions of roaches who are willing to fight for truth, justice and the cockroach way!"

I could see his chest swell with pride. The little "S" on his blue and red outfit started to expand. But just then a little girl came in to the restaurant and spotted us talking.

"Look, mother," she said. "Up on the wall. It's an ant . . . it's a termite . . . it's Super Roach."

And with that dozens of exterminators swooped into the building with spray guns of insecticide.

"Sorry to cut this interview short, lady," Super Roach called over his shoulder. "But I've got to split. See you in Florida next year!"

34
There's no solution
to the jigsaw puzzle

There's nothing like a jigsaw puzzle to keep a family on its toes.

Once the pieces are spread across the dining room table, there's not much of a choice. You have to eat standing up or you don't eat at all.

I thought it would be fun to give my 11-year-old daughter a jigsaw puzzle for Christmas last year.

"This is great," she said as she dumped 700 tiny pieces across the living room floor on Christmas morning.

Seeing the dog pick up one of the pieces and head behind the sofa, I started dumping the puzzle back in the box and said, "Why don't we wait for some day that's a little less hectic before we start this project, dear?"

Two days later my daughter appropriated the dining room table, and it was occupied for months.

It took her a week to form the border of the puzzle, which shows a cute little white dog on a dark green background. It was just plain agony. The fact that two-thirds of the puzzle is solid green and the other third is solid white didn't help.

When all the outside pieces were put in place and it was time to work on the hard part, she seemed to lose interest.

Here was my golden opportunity, and I blew it. Instead of dumping all 700 pieces into the garbage can, I sat down at the table and tried to fill in a few holes.

At that instant the jigsaw puzzle became a family project, and we were morally committed to completing the white dog on the dark green background.

And as with all family projects, it was nearly impossible to get my daughter to participate.

"Let's all get together tonight and work on that puzzle," I would say as we sat on the floor eating breakfast.

"I think I'm going to have homework to do tonight, Mom. Why don't you and Dad work on it by yourselves."

The one person in our house who really had the desire to work on the puzzle was our 6-year-old. She picked up piece after piece, put them on the table, and hammered them together with her little fist. Too bad she never matched up two pieces that actually belonged together.

As the weeks went by, the puzzle began to take shape. We finally found the dog's nose under the sofa, and part of his ear on the kitchen counter behind the bread box.

I suspect our own dog ate the piece that showed the puzzle dog's eye. We never did find it.

Finally last week the puzzle was complete (with the exception of the one eye).

When you're finished with a jigsaw puzzle, you have three choices. You can mount it on cardboard with glue, then hang it on the wall. Or you can leave it on the table for a few months so everyone can admire your work.

My husband chose Plan 3. He dumped all 700 pieces back in the box as fast as he could while we all stood around, watching in horror.

"Tonight, we're going to sit down for dinner," he said.

We all learned a lesson from the jigsaw puzzle experience.

My daughters learned that perseverance pays off. My husband learned that it was possible to eat sitting on the floor. And I learned not to buy another jigsaw puzzle until we have a house with a playroom or a basement.

113

35
Cars are auto-matic trouble

I truly envy people who are mechanically minded.

The only thing I understand about a car is that if you push down on the gas pedal, it somehow makes the wheels go faster. I know that there is something called an engine in between the gas pedal and the wheels, but I don't have the faintest idea how or why it works.

The reason I know there is an engine is because one time I accidentally lifted the hood up and caught a glimpse of a bunch of tubes, a mess of wires and a lot of dirt. I quickly closed the hood and vowed never to look again.

And I've kept that promise.

When something goes wrong with my car, I make a beeline for my favorite gas station. I just describe the symptom, ask for a ride home and tell them to give me a call when the car works again.

The people at my gas station know that I've put my car's life in their hands. They take good care of me.

Their attitude is refreshing, I might add. I've been to plenty of garages and car maintenance shops where the employees treat you like a dirty spark plug, whatever that is.

You walk in and wait at the front desk to explain what is wrong with your car. The man behind the desk never even looks up to acknowledge your presence. He obviously hopes that by ignoring you, you will go away.

When you finally succeed in capturing his attention, he makes you feel like a kid reporting to the principal's office.

"What do you mean there's a rattle in the radiator?"

"Just what makes you think that there's something wrong with the transmission?"

"Are you sure you weren't just pushing on the gas pedal and the brake pedal at the same time?"

After finally convincing the man at the front desk that there is indeed something wrong with your car, you have to put up with the mechanics, who do their best to intimidate you and make you feel like a certified nincompoop.

"Why haven't you changed this oil for three years?"

"If you don't take better care of this car, it's gonna fall apart right on your garage floor."

"Lady, don't you know the difference between a squeal and a screech?"

None of this happens at my gas station. They know how stupid I am when it comes to cars, but they treat me like a princess anyway.

If I tell them it sounds like there's a frog in the speedometer, they don't laugh in my face. They always turn their backs, thinking I won't see them laughing. Now that's consideration.

And talk about service! The other day my car stalled about eight blocks away from my gas station. Naturally, I gave them a call and they came running.

"Maybe the battery is dead," I said. That's about the limit of my car problem lingo.

They took my car to the station where they gave everything a quick check. About 20 minutes later I got a call at home.

"I found your problem, Debby."

"Was it a dead battery?"

"No, you were out of gas."

I heard laughter in the background and I knew my reputation had hit a new low. Searching frantically for an excuse, I heard myself saying "I know. I was just testing you guys. Good work."

36
Sew what else is new?

Sooner or later the Women's Movement has got to tackle alterations.

For years the stores have been charging women for the same service they give away free to men. If that isn't blatant discrimination, I don't know what is!

I've always just assumed that when men got alterations on their clothes, they had to pay extra just like women. But last month I found out the awful truth.

I happened to be with my husband when he was looking for a new suit.

"How do you like this one?" he asked, stuffing his arms in a brown suit that looked about three sizes too big.

Before I could tell him how ridiculous he looked, a salesman came running over and started complimenting my husband on his fine choice.

"This shade of brown is perfect for you," the salesman said as he patted down the shoulders and smoothed out the sleeves. "It looks really great."

I could tell that my husband liked the way this conversation was going, but he was not blind.

"Do you have the same suit in a smaller size?" he asked.

The salesman routed through the racks but came up empty-handed.

"It looks like this is the only one we have, but we can shorten the sleeves a bit and pull in the waist and it will look just dandy. Let me call in our tailor."

In no time at all my husband was standing in front of a full-length mirror and a tailor was marking up the suit with a little piece of chalk.

"Pull in the shoulders two inches," he mumbled. "Bring up the sleeves an inch. Move the buttons over. Shorten the coat. Pull in the waist. Cut here. Slice there."

And all the while he was wielding that little piece of chalk like a butcher uses his knife to slice up a side of beef. When the tailor was done, my husband looked like the blackboard in my high school geometry class. I thought he was going to need an eraser to get all the chalk marks off.

"Thanks very much," the salesman told my husband after the tailor finishing his diagramming. "You can pick up your suit on Tuesday."

"By the time they get through slicing that suit up and stitching it back together, you're going to end up with a pretty expensive set of threads," I told him.

That's when he explained that men aren't charged for alterations when they buy clothes. I couldn't believe what I was hearing.

The last time I went shopping for clothes, it took me hours to find a dress that I liked. I hunted down a sales clerk, held up the dress and said "I'd like to try this on. How do you think it will look?"

"Forget it, honey," she said, as she looked up from painting her nails.

I practically had to beg them to let me use the dressing room.

"One item at a time, lady," the guard outside the dressing room shouted. "And we require you to leave your purse, your watch, and your first-born child with me, just to make sure you don't try to steal anything while you're inside the dressing room."

Ignoring the smirks and catty remarks from the clerk who was posted inside the dressing room, I decided to buy the dress.

"Which way is the fitting room?" I asked the guard as I collected my things.

"Can't you read?" she said, pointing to a sign on the wall next to the door to the fitting room.

I went through the door, looked around, and said in a timid voice, "Pardon me, but is this the fitting room?"

A stout woman looked up at me and said "Whaddu want?" I could tell by the tone of her voice that she had spit a lot of needles in her lifetime.

"I'd like to get this dress shortened a bit."

She pointed to a platform. I climbed up the little step. She motioned me to turn around. I obeyed. Then she started sticking little pins into the bottom of the dress and into my leg.

"Don't you think it should be a little shorter?" I asked her.

She just grunted and stuck me with another pin.

When she was through, she pointed her finger toward the dressing room, which was her way of telling me to get out of her life.

"When can I pick up the dress?" I asked the clerk as she was adding a $10 alteration fee to the bill.

She looked at her calendar. "Maybe next month, if the seamstress gets caught up. Give us a call in three weeks and I'll let you know if it's done."

Where is Gloria Steinam when you really need her?

37
How to survive a vacation

Despite the fact that tourism officials are paying thousands of dollars on advertising brochures to lure folks to Florida in the summer, I spend my summer months pouring over pictures of mountain retreats, streams and cool lakes, apple orchards and scenic country roads.

The problem with vacations is that the anticipation is always so much better than the actual trip.

I never have any trouble conjuring up a picture of my family frolicking in a cool mountain lake, with a comfortable cabin in the background and a warm glow from the campfire.

To get there, however, you've got to stick a family of four into a small car and send them out on the open road. That's when reality takes over, and the true test of family compatability begins.

I'll never forget our last family vacation. What interesting places we visited.

We spent one very long night at Eazy Ed's Muffler Repair in Marietta, Ga. We enjoyed a blistering hot afternoon at Savannah Tire and Wheel. The highlight of the trip was the two entertaining days we spent in the customer's lounge of Tommy's Transmission in Charlotte, N.C. What a selection of reading material they had!

I've found that deciding on a place to stay is one of the biggest challenges of any vacation. When I think of hotels, places like The Breakers or The Greenbrier come to mind.

119

My idea of roughing it is when the hotel maid turns down my bed at night and forgets to leave a little chocolate mint on the pillow.

My husband's idea of overnight accommodations is anything under $20. That pretty much limits us to tents, log cabins and those 1950-type motels that are painted pink and have an Edsel parked out front.

I'm sure you've all seen them. Inside, there's one Danish Modern chair, two lumpy mattresses hidden under faded orange bedspreads, and a paint-by-number picture of a sailboat at sunset nailed to the wall. The black and white TV set gets only one channel, which features Smurfs and "snow" 24 hours-a-day.

Knowing that we might be staying in such luxurious quarters, I always pack an extra suitcase filled with ant-and-roach killer, "real" toilet paper, Lysol spray, two or three clean towels and enough slippers to ensure that nobody's feet will ever have to touch the dirty floor. I forgot to include the calculator my husband carries along to add up how much he's saved by steering clear of those $100-a-night hotels.

If he's in a **really** cheap mood, we stay with friends or relatives along the way. That's always good for free room and board, but you sometimes have to endure hours of boring conversation and endless tours of the new mall in town. And it's no picnic spending the night with your kids crammed in a sofa bed in an un-air conditioned attic in July.

I have a feeling that the days of mooching off relatives are over for us. The last time we stayed at cousin Albert's house, my husband spent three days of his vacation helping Albert paint his house. I loved it!

Meals are another problem on a vacation trip. To save time (and money) our family lugs along a cooler in the car. That makes good sense during the first day. But by the time you hit Atlanta and your luncheon choice is soggy peanut butter and jelly or smelly tunafish, even the kids

lose their appetites.

Despite the little trouble spots on the road to a happy vacation, you do get to meet interesting people along the way. Like the waitress in Charleston who spilled her guts about her miserable marriage while we were trying to eat our dessert. Or the 85-year-old doctor who told me our children had a rare skin disease when all they really had was poison ivy. Or the friendly drunk who backed into our car in Jacksonville. Or the policeman who arrested us for backing up on the interstate exit we had mistakenly used.

With such memories, I don't know why I still long for

another vacation.

"I know this sounds crazy," I told my husband last summer, "but let's hop in the car and go to the mountains for a few days. Wouldn't it be great to take a little vacation?"

"You've got a vacation coming up . . . a nine-month vacation," he said. "As soon as the kids are back in school, your vacation begins."

If he's that confused, he needs a vacation more than I do!

Another copy?

Wouldn't you like to send a little slice of paradise to your friends and relatives? What better way to let them know what Florida is all about than by sending copies of Debby Wood's book.

Simply fill out the order blank below, and send a check for $4.95 per copy, or three books for $13, plus 80 cents postage and handling for each book ordered. (Florida residents must add 5 percent state sales tax. That's 25 cents per book.)

If you want the books sent directly to your friends or relatives, please print the name, address and zip code legibly on a piece of paper and send it along with your order.

Send the order to: Debby Wood, Box 1737, Cape Coral, FL 33910.